The Gypsies Never Came

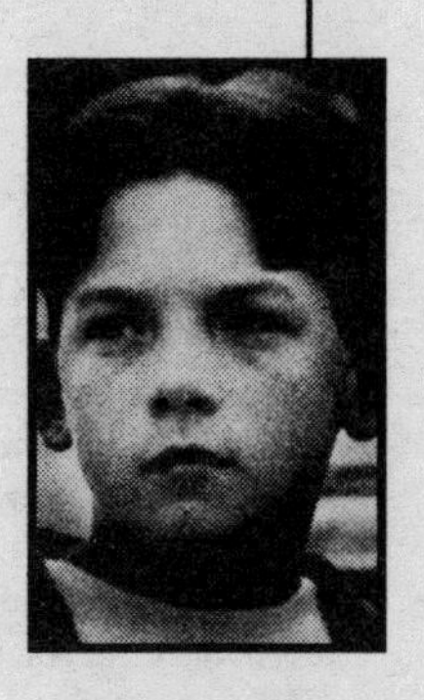

The Gypsies Never Came

Stephen Roos

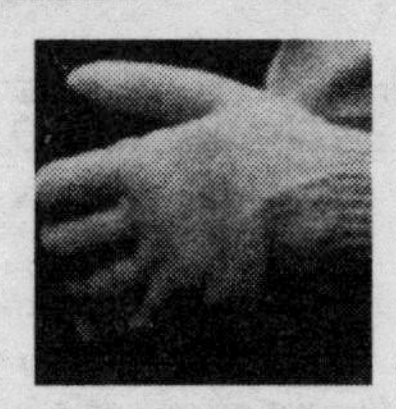

ALADDIN PAPERBACKS

New York London Toronto Sydney Singapore

First Aladdin Paperbacks edition December 2002

ALADDIN PAPERBACKS
An imprint of Simon & Schuster
Children's Publishing Division
1230 Avenue of the Americas
New York, NY 10020

Also available in a Simon & Schuster Books for Young Readers hardcover edition.
Designed by Anahid Hamparian
The text of this book was set in 12 Point Dutch 766.

Printed and bound in the United States of America
2 4 6 8 10 9 7 5 3 1

The Library of Congress has cataloged the hardcover edition as follows:
Roos, Stephen.
The Gypsies never came/by Stephen Roos.
p. cm.
Summary: Sixth-grader Augie Knapp, who has a deformed hand, is convinced by Lydie Rose, the strange new girl in town, that the Gypsies are coming for him.
[1. Physically handicapped—Fiction. 2. Schools—Fiction. 3. Self-acceptance—Fiction.]
I. Title.
Pz7.R6753 Gy 2001
[Fic]—dc21 99-058951
ISBN 0-689-83147-1 (hc.)
ISBN 0-689-85309-2 (Aladdin pbk.)

For all the Gypsies

There is always one moment in childhood when the door opens and lets the future in.

—Graham Greene, *The Power and the Glory*

The Gypsies Never Came

Chapter One

IT'S EARLY. The sun is barely clearing the eastern ridge.

Augie Knapp stands under the leafless oak in the Warnkes' backyard. There's still snow on the ground, but he's wearing an undershirt and cutoffs, like it's the middle of July.

On his left hand is a flesh-colored glove. The other hand is bare.

"Kyle? You awake yet?"

Like anyone could sleep through Augie's frogular croak. "Kyle! Come look!"

Finally, a light goes on upstairs.

The window flies open. A head leans out. "What the heck are you doing, Augie?"

"Freezing my buns off." Augie laughs. "What's it look like I'm doing?"

"Go back to bed and get some sleep, why don't you?" Kyle groans.

"Been there, done that," Augie shouts back.

But Kyle's already slammed the window shut.

Augie leaps onto the lattice. Grabbing the cross-slats

with his right hand, he hoists himself up the side of the Warnkes' house. When he reaches the second story, he sees Kyle on the other side of the glass. "Open up!"

Kyle shakes his head. "No way!" he mouths.

"I'll wake everyone in the neighborhood!" Augie croaks as he raps on the glass with the gloved hand.

Slowly, Kyle opens the window again. "Give me a break, Augie. Let me get a little more sleep before school."

"You don't need more sleep. It's March twenty-first. It's the first day of spring, Kyle. We need to go up the ridge and find out where the stream begins."

"It's still winter," Kyle tells him. "The stream's still frozen, you jerk!"

Augie hears wood crack. He feels the lattice giving way under him. "Help me!" he cries.

Kyle reaches out and tries to grab him. Too late. The thin strips of wood are collapsing too fast.

Augie's arms flail at the sill, at the TV cable, at anything to break his fall. Something catches the end of Augie's arm. He crashes to the ground. The wind knocked out of him, Augie lies spread-eagled in the snow. As he looks up, he sees Kyle leaning over the windowsill, his face scrunched up with worry.

"Oh, gosh, Augie!" he shouts. "Are you hurt?"

"Don't know yet," Augie gasps.

"But you're not dead or anything, are you?"

"Don't think so." He sees the glove. It's dangling on a nail. Suddenly his little smile evaporates. "My glove!" he cries out, sitting up suddenly.

"I can do that," Kyle says. "Wait till I . . ."

As Augie gets to his feet, he instinctively tucks his left

arm behind him, out of Kyle's sight. He makes a jump for the glove, then another. The nail's too high up.

He spots a snow shovel on the porch. Grabbing it with his good hand, he hurls the shovel into the air. It hits the side of the house, nudging the glove off the offending nail.

Kyle opens the front door. The legs of his red flannel pajamas tucked into his snow boots, he bolts onto the porch. "Let me help," he says.

"Got it," Augie says, picking the glove off the top of the snow.

"Come in, Augie. Get warm," Kyle says. "Maybe we can go up the ridge later, if you feel like it."

Shaking his head, Augie picks up the glove, examining it. It's all messed up. The fingers are ripped up, and the cotton stuffing's falling out. "I got to get home before my mom goes down to the beer company," he says anxiously. "She's going to be mad. I know it."

With his good hand he leans what's left of the lattice and Kyle's mom's wisteria against the house. Then he heads home.

Augie steps in from the cold. He breathes in the kitchen-warm smells of coffee mingling with burned toast.

Uncle Emil sits at the table. He's in his U.S. Postal Service uniform, drinking his coffee. "What were you doing outside in that getup?" he asks, shaking his head.

"It's spring," Augie says with a shrug. "Doesn't *any-one* around here ever look at a calendar?"

"You're sure one funny kid," Emil says, sighing, "and I don't mean funny ha-ha, either."

"Don't mind him, Augie," Augie's mom says as she grabs Emil's mug.

"Hey, Honey, I wasn't through," Emil protests.

"That's what you get for calling Augie funny," she says as she dumps what's left of Emil's coffee in the sink.

Anyone can tell Uncle Emil and Honey are brother and sister. They have the same blond hair, same ruddy complexion. She's just a lot younger than he is. Wearing her Grateful Dead T-shirt and a denim skirt that barely reaches her knees, she could pass for a high school kid.

(Sometimes, when she's acting more like a kid than a mom, Augie calls her by her first name. She doesn't seem to mind, as long as no one's around.)

"You hurry, Augie," his mom says, pointing to the orange juice and cereal waiting for him on the table. "You don't want to be late for school." She closes the dishwasher door and turns the dial. The dishwasher thumps heavily into action.

"Mom?"

But the dishwasher's too loud. He knows she can't hear him. "Mom?" he asks, louder this time. Augie dangles the glove in the air. This time he catches her eye.

"Oh, Augie," she groans. "How?"

"It got caught on a nail."

"A nail?" she asks suspiciously.

"Don't blame me if people leave nails where they shouldn't," Augie says.

"When are you going to that clinic over in Greenburgh?" Uncle Emil asks.

"That place is for amputees," Augie protests. "I already told you."

"They can still fit you with a hook, Augie," Uncle Emil

says. "I checked. Free of charge, too. Government pays the whole thing."

Augie feels the blood rushing to his face. "I'm not like those people."

"Augie, I'm just trying—"

"You don't tell me what to do," Augie protests. "You're not my father."

Emil grabs his coat from the hook by the back door. "If you got yourself a hook, you wouldn't need that silly glove," he says. "That's all I'm saying."

"Please, Emil," Honey pleads. "Not now."

Once Emil's gone, Honey takes a box from the cupboard. Inside are half a dozen left-hand gloves like the one Augie just ruined, plus a bag of cotton balls and another bag full of wire pieces.

"Do it later," Augie tells her. "You don't have to be late for the beer company."

"You plan to keep your hand in your pocket all day?" she asks as she makes up his new glove.

He looks at the little ball of pink flesh at the end of his wrist. On it are little bumps of cartilage where the fingers were supposed to grow.

"Just in the morning," Augie says. "At lunch, I'll take it out and watch the kids barf all over the place."

"Augie, you shouldn't talk like that."

"It's a joke." Augie shrugs. "I'm being funny."

"Funny ha-ha or funny the other way?" she asks.

Augie crosses his eyes and lets a little spit drool down his chin. "Can't someone be both?" he asks, putting on the new glove.

Chapter Two

TAPED TO the green tile walls are drawings of teeth that like to be brushed after every meal and hands that need to be washed with soap before they leave the bathroom. It's too dumb for sixth grade, but Miss Merkel says leave them up. It's better than bare walls, she says.

Augie sits at the end of the far row. From his corner, he can see everyone. One row over, Blue Tebaldo, the only sixth grader this year with blue hair, is drawing horses. Two rows ahead, Cupper Marks is passing a note to Bren Goody. Kyle's finishing the math homework that's due before lunch.

Miss Merkel's at the blackboard, diagramming a sentence. Even if she's about to retire, she doesn't look all that old. Just tired. If Augie had known it was going to be subjects and predicates again, he would have sneaked in a horror story like Denny Swoboda one row over, three rows down.

"When's safety patrol elections, Miss Merkel?" Marty Kuhlman asks.

(Marty's the best athlete. He has the best clothes, too.

Augie even got Honey to buy him the same Nikes that Marty has.)

"What's safety patrol got to do with English, Marty?" Miss Merkel asks.

"Well, it's the last time," Marty says. "They don't have safety patrol in junior high."

Miss Merkel rests the chalk in the tray. "How about the day after tomorrow?" she suggests. "You can nominate anybody but the kids who have been safety patrol already."

(That means Denny Swoboda, and Bren Goody, and Toby Engel. Every year they get elected to everything.)

"Who's going to nominate you, Marty?" E. Banacek asks.

"What makes you think I'm even running?"

"Well, duh—"

"I'm nominating him," Denny Swoboda interrupts.

Miss Merkel picks up the chalk and starts diagramming again.

"Miss Merkel?"

It's Ginger Izbicki. She sits next seat over from Augie. Twisting her hair in her fingers like always and wearing sweats that are probably hand-me-downs from her brothers.

"Yes, Ginger?" Miss Merkel replies, but she keeps right on diagramming.

"Is it okay to nominate yourself?"

Most of the kids laugh. Augie included. No matter how thick those sweats are, anyone can see right through her.

"Someone's got to nominate you," E. Banacek says.

"I was asking Miss Merkel," Ginger says, staring at the floor.

"Well, I'm right. Aren't I, Miss Merkel?" E. asks.

This time, Miss Merkel drops her chalk in the tray. "There's no law says you can't nominate yourself," she says.

"Only no one ever does nominate themself," E. goes on.

"Himself," Miss Merkel says. "Or herself. Or themselves. There's no such word as 'themself.'"

"Whatever," E. says agreeably. E. turns around in her chair. "If you want to run, Ginger, you should probably get Blue to nominate you," she says.

"Blue?" Ginger asks. "Why him?"

"Well, you guys eat lunch together," E. says.

"Nerd table!" Chris Garelik shouts.

"We don't talk like that here, Chris," Miss Merkel says before the giggles get out of hand.

Ginger leans forward in her seat. "You want to, Blue?" she asks.

Blue looks up from his drawing. "Safety patrol's a joke," he announces.

"Better get someone else to nominate you," E. says. "Maybe you should *pay* someone!"

"Drop dead, you stupid busybody," Ginger says, and in a very loud voice, too.

Miss Merkel wraps the pointer on her desk before it gets out of hand. Looking even wearier than she did five minutes before, she goes back to her diagramming. Blue goes back to his drawing. Denny goes back to his horror story. Bren Goody is secretly reading the note from Cupper Marks, and it looks like Kyle has finally finished his math homework.

Ginger leans over toward Augie.

"Yeah?" he asks.

"You know how much it costs to get someone to nominate you?" she whispers.

Chapter Three

THE CAGE rattles ferociously. Mr. Claude McPhee's camel hair topcoat swings in its plastic bag as Augie pedals the trike over the speed bump at the end of Mission Lane.

The trike is three times the size of a kid's trike. The cage is four feet tall. It's wedged between the two back wheels. Mrs. Lumaghi's son-in-law Rudy made it mostly from aluminum oven racks he scavenged on Metal Monday at the transfer station. Rudy made the sign, too.

Lumaghi Cleaners
Free Delivery
555-3291

The letters are red and green on a white background. It's the same colors as the Italian flag. If Augie had a nickel for every time someone asked for extra cheese on their laundry, he'd be a millionaire.

As he hits a pothole, the cage rattles even louder. Augie looks over his shoulder. Claude McPhee's overcoat is lying on the bottom of the cage.

He pulls the bike to the curb. Goes around to the back. Opens the cage. Puts the coat back on its hanger. Puts the hanger on the rod. Closes the cage. (Can't be too careful. Mrs. Lumaghi's got her spies everywhere. They're all a hundred years old, but their eyes are good. One of them is probably sneaking a peek right now.)

The cold wind picks up. As Augie zips up his jacket, he spots some yellow scratch paper in the gutter. It's all crumpled up, like someone couldn't wait to get rid of it.

He glances at the men talking in front of the hardware store. A teenage girl is wheeling a baby carriage into Krulis-Hallmark. Augie scoops the paper up, but he doesn't look until he's back on the trike.

Eggs

Toilet paper

Comet

Just some dumb shopping list. Augie's bugged. What's the point in antilittering laws if no one enforces them?

The girl with the carriage is looking at him. He doesn't care. He stuffs the list into his pocket, pedals past where the old hardware store used to be, past the diner, past the movie theater that closed two years ago.

Main Street is only three blocks long. But just about all the stores and offices that haven't moved out to the mall are here. One or two stories tall, the buildings are brick, mostly. The elms that grew on both sides of the street died before Augie was born, and no one has gotten around to planting anything new.

The only tall building is Mozart Hall. It's five

stories. They built it when the coal mines were being worked and Warsaw Junction was supposed to become a city. It was supposed to be for concerts. Now half of it is a gym, and the other half belongs to the Benevolent Order of Beavers.

Augie leaves the trike on the sidewalk and takes Mr. McPhee's topcoat from the cage. As he steps inside, the little bell above the door tinkles. The air is tight and hot, heavy with the sweet, industrial smell of dry-cleaning fluid. The posters of the Colosseum in Rome, a Venetian canal, and the Amalfi coast are faded now, and cracked.

"Hi, Mrs. Lumaghi!"

She stands at the pink Formica counter, waiting on Mr. Lebo from the bank. Without looking up, she nods in Augie's direction, saying nothing.

She's an old woman. Her hair is all white, and she doesn't wear lipstick or earrings. When Augie stands close, he smells talcum powder.

Mrs. Lumaghi rings up the sale. Mumbling to herself, she counts out the change. "You brought the camel back?" she asks, looking up at him finally.

"I waited," he explains.

"How long?"

"Five minutes," he says.

"I bet."

"Almost," he admits. "I went around back. I went next door, too."

Mrs. Lumaghi scowls. "I got no time to argue, my friend," she says, waving an impatient hand in the air.

"But I did try," he says.

"I got to sit down, Augie." She sighs.

"You sick?" he asks.

"My legs," she explains. "Dr. Jaleel says I got very close veins, Augie."

She pushes aside the curtain behind her and waddles painfully to the back of the store. As Montel's theme music comes up, Augie begins to pick through the pile of clothes behind the counter.

After the deliveries, it's his job to empty the pockets before Mrs. Lumaghi puts the dirty clothes in the dry-cleaning machine. Mostly it's candy wrappers, and some small change, and a ton of used Kleenex. The end of cold and flu season, Augie's got to expect that, Mrs. Lumaghi tells him.

Augie's halfway through a lady's brown tweed jacket before he finds anything decent. It's a letter. Hand-written, too; the writing is so small, it takes forever to decipher whom it's to.

Gray Dmytryck
148 Chestnut Street
Warsaw Junction, PA

Everyone in Warsaw Junction knows Gray Dmytryck. She's the mayor's wife. She's supposed to drink. A lot, too. He overheard Mr. Preston at the "Pump and Pay" say she went to someplace for it but it didn't do any good and now she's worse than before.

He slips the letter out of the envelope. His back to the front of the store, he leans against the counter and begins to read it.

Dear Gray,

The next time you come around for money, try

The bell!

As soon as he hears it, he jumps. He jams the letter into his pocket. The envelope flutters to the linoleum floor. Hastily he picks it up and shoves it in his pocket, too.

She's wearing an old lady cloth coat. It's one of Mrs. Lumaghi's cronies, but he can't tell which one. The brim of the black straw hat is too wide to see the face under it.

As she dumps a pile of clothes on the counter, she tilts her head back. She's no old lady. She's tall, but she's just a kid! No one he ever saw before. Skin as white as chalk. Narrow slits for eyeholes. Hardly any lips. Wisps of curly red hair sticking out from under the brim.

"Two dresses, a sweater, my jacket."

She talks fast. Very high and breathy. Augie writes it down on the receipt.

"Is your hand cold?" she asks.

He looks up. Her eyes are on the hand with the glove. Without a word, Augie shoves the gloved hand in his pocket.

"Nice watch," the girl says. "You know where I can get me one?"

"Name?" he asks sourly as he takes a pencil from the mug by the register.

"Lydie Rose," she states. Just as friendly as can be, too. If she's noticed the tone of Augie's voice, she's doing a good job pretending otherwise.

He writes "Lydie" where the first name goes. He writes "Rose" where the last name goes.

"Meisenheimer," she says.

"Huh?"

"That's my last name."

"But I already wrote 'Rose' where the last name is

supposed to go," he says. "You want me to start all over?"

"It'd be easier than changing my last name," she points out.

"Easier for you, maybe," Augie grunts.

Grabbing another receipt, he scribbles something with an "M" at the beginning and an "R" at the end and a long, wiggly line in between. He's not about to ask how she spells that last name of hers.

The sooner he gets rid of this one, the sooner he can go back to Gray Dmytryck's letter. "They should be ready in two days," he says, handing her the new, improved receipt for her crummy clothes.

"Can I keep this till then?" Lydie Rose Meisenheimer asks.

"Keep what?"

She dangles a watch in front of his eyes, like a hypnotist sending someone into a trance.

"Hey, is that . . . ?" He checks his wrist. "That's my watch! How did you—?"

"Just something an old Gypsy taught me," Lydie Rose says. "You want me to show you?"

"You want me to call the cops on you?"

She tosses him the watch. Then she unbuttons her old lady coat and tosses it on the counter. "Can you clean this, too?" she asks.

Did someone open a thrift shop just for old lady clothes? Under her old lady coat, Lydie Rose is wearing the flimsiest old lady dress Augie ever saw. It's black, no sleeves, with big pink cabbage roses all the way down to her tennis shoes with their neon green laces.

"You want to freeze when you get outside?" he asks her.

"But it's the twenty-first!" Lydie Rose exclaims. "Who could be cold the first day of spring?"

The little bell tinkles as she leaves.

Augie shakes his head. So what if no one else but her and him care if it's spring? She's got to be the most outlandish piece of work that ever marched herself and her dirty old clothes into Mrs. Lumaghi's. People like that don't last long around Warsaw Junction. You got to be glad for that, don't you?

Through the plate glass he watches Lydie Rose wander down Main Street like it's sixty degrees out. An old, mangy dog limps along after her. He checks his wrist again, just to make sure the watch is still there.

Chapter Four

"I GOT A batch of new cards," his mom says. "You want to check them out?"

"Guess so," he says.

The drawer under the counter is crammed with his mom's stuff. Augie practically has to pry it open. It's got old lipsticks. Hair clips. Girl things. Scrunchies.

But mostly it's Honey's card collection. She stops by Krulis-Hallmark, right across from Mrs. Lumaghi's, once a week, sometimes twice, and she never comes out empty-handed.

The overflow falls to the floor. Cards, mostly, but some photographs.

"Hey, look at me!" his mom yells, pointing to a color shot.

It's her in a bathing suit, looking over her shoulder at the camera. Her blond hair is halfway down her back. That's why they call her Honey, on account of her hair.

"I must have been fifteen," his mom says, examining the photo more closely.

Augie notices another photograph. It's a man on a

horse. His hair's so black, it almost shines. "Who's that?"

"Who?" Augie holds the snapshot out to her. "His hair's like mine," he says.

She grabs the card out of his hand, stuffing it in her pocket. "It's no one," she says.

Like it didn't happen. So Augie acts like it didn't happen, too.

He scoops the cards up from the floor and puts them on the kitchen table. Birthday. Anniversary. Congratulations. Get Well Soon. We Miss You. Happy Retirement. Hardly anyone in Warsaw Junction has an occasion without his mom sending them a card.

Augie checks one of the new ones.

Happy Anniversary,
Sweetheart!
If I had it to do
all over again,

Turn inside:

I'd
do it
all over
YOU!

It really cracks him up.

"I got it for you," his mom says.

"How come?" he asks.

"It's so stupid," Honey says. "I knew it would make you laugh."

He goes through the rest. "Cheer Up." "Smile." "Look for That Sky of Blue."

"Who's this for?" he asks, holding up "Tomorrow Is Another Day."

"Someone having a hard time," she says.

"Like they've got an incurable disease?"

"I don't know anyone like that," his mom admits.

"How about psychos?"

His mom arches an eyebrow. "Here in Warsaw Junction?" she asks.

"What about prune-face next door?" Augie asks.

"Don't say that. Mrs. Hamblin's a nice lady."

"I guess being a psycho isn't exactly an occasion," Augie goes on. "It's not like flunking sixth grade or getting a divorce."

"Hallmark don't have cards for that."

"Well, they should," Augie croaks. "They should have a whole line of cards for that. Sorry You Flunked Sixth Grade. Sorry You Lost Your Job. Sorry No One Can Stand You. Sorry You're a Total Screwup."

"Oh, Augie," Honey says. "It's not funny."

"Is too!" He laughs.

"It's just mean!" Honey protests. "You're not going to make me laugh."

But of course, he is. He can count on it. Every time. It takes a moment, but soon she's laughing so hard, the tears are streaming down her cheeks.

"You got another card," she says, wiping her face finally. "I almost forgot."

"From you?"

Shaking her head, she points to the envelope on the lazy Susan. It has his name on it, too. Big, messy letters like a little kid wrote it out.

"Where did that come from?" he asks.

"Ginger dropped it off," she tells him.

Augie grabs an apple from the plastic bowl next to the toaster.

"Aren't you going to open it?"

"Sure," Augie says.

"When?"

"When I feel like it," Augie tells her.

"Maybe it's a love letter, Augie," his mom teases.

"I kind of doubt it," Augie says.

"You're cute," Honey says. "Why not?"

"Don't make me throw up," he says, tossing the apple core in the garbage. He grabs the envelope and heads out to the barn. The last thing he's going to do is open anything personal in front of Honey.

Uncle Emil hasn't had a horse since before Augie was born, but there's still hay in the barn. Augie smells it as he gropes his way across the fallen beams and rotten shingles and tree limbs.

The winter before was the ice storm. The oak in the backyard fell, totaling the barn. Next year, if there's enough money, Uncle Emil's hiring men to tear the whole thing down and cart it away.

Till then Augie has it to himself. He doesn't like to think what he'll do when it's gone. A key hangs from a hook in the farthest stall. It's the only place where the roof didn't cave yet. Kneeling in the far corner, Augie pushes away some hay. The suitcase is buried under a foot of it.

(The suitcase is his secret. Even Kyle doesn't know about it.)

It's almost filled now. Augie's got letters and notes.

Postcards. Alaska. Chicago. Mexico. He's got the matches Mr. Fountain left in the faculty can and the pink slip Miss Merkel's sister got from the phone company. He's even got Benno Kelly's report card from fifth grade. Every time he looks at it he smiles a little. Augie never saw grades so bad. No wonder Benno didn't take that home!

He picks up a card. On the front is a big Christmas tree, all lit up, with a mom and a dad, four kids, and a big yellow dog, sort of a Lab and husky mix.

Seasons Greetings

FROM

The Wyatts

Bob and Dorothy

Debby, Laurel, Tommy, and Bobby, Jr.

and Clem

Everyone's grinning for the camera, like they mean it, too. Even the dog. Augie figures that's got to be Clem. He loves looking at this card. It was in a book about Mayans that Uncle Emil got from the library.

At first he'd pretend he was little Tommy. Now that he's twelve, he's Bobby, Jr. It doesn't make a difference, really. Wyatts are perfect.

He's looking at the Wyatts so hard, he almost forgets the envelope his mom gave him. He rips it open. No letter. He double-checks. Not even scratch paper with something mean written on it.

Just a ten-dollar bill.

As he sticks it in the suitcase, he remembers the letter he found at Mrs. Lumaghi's that afternoon. "The next time you come around for money . . ." It was to Gray Dmytryck, the mayor's wife.

What happened to it?

It should be here. Somewhere.

But it's not.

He hadn't finished the first sentence before that weird girl interrupted him. Then he came home, and he went through Honey's cards, and he found the ten bucks from Ginger. And that's all he remembers.

Back in his room, he looks under his bed. And in the wastebasket by his desk. He checks the windbreaker that's hanging on a hook in the kitchen, just in case.

But it's gone.

Chapter Five

MOST DAYS, if the weather is okay, Augie and Kyle walk to JFK Middle together. It's a long walk when the weather is rotten.

Today it isn't. Overnight, the mountain air has lost its winter sting. The snow has melted into puddles. As Augie's shoes sink into the soft ground, he can almost smell the black earth heating up.

Kyle's wearing his new baseball cap. It's a Pirates cap. No big surprise. Pittsburgh's only a couple hours. Even if everyone in Warsaw Junction has a different reason for hating Pittsburgh, that's the team they root for around here.

"You should push the brim to the back," Augie tells him. "Like this." He swivels the cap around on Kyle's head.

"How come?"

"It's how they wear baseball caps."

"Who?"

"Kids."

"It's not how baseball players wear them," Kyle

says, swiveling the brim back over his face.

Augie's just trying to help. Sometimes Augie doesn't know why he bothers.

Elections are tomorrow. Just in case anyone's forgotten, Miss Merkel writes it on the blackboard.

Safety Patrol Elections
Tomorrow

"What *time* tomorrow?" Ginger asks. "Before lunch or after?"

"I'll decide that tomorrow," Miss Merkel says.

"Whatever," Ginger says. "Just as long as we have them." She turns toward Augie. "You going to do it?" she whispers.

"Maybe," he says, shrugging.

"You'd better, Augie," she warns him. "If you know what's good for you."

Monday and Friday, when the class does gymnastics for Mr. Shimkus, Augie goes to the faculty lounge. It usually takes him an hour to do all the photocopying Mrs. McCann's secretary leaves for him.

Except for when Augie found Mr. Fountain smoking in the faculty can, photocopying's worse than diagramming sentences.

Today, while he makes copies of next week's menu, Mrs. Zuckerman and Mrs. Battle are sitting on the couch, gossiping like he isn't there. Mrs. Zuckerman is new this year. Augie had Mrs. Battle for first grade.

Mrs. Battle is telling Mrs. Zuckerman about the

dinner she and her husband had at Ligonier Tavern on Saturday night.

"You wouldn't believe the servings," she exclaims. "Talk about getting the biggest bang for your buck!"

"Did Harold like it?" Mrs. Zuckerman asks.

"Oh, he'll eat anything and everything," Mrs. Battle replies. "That man would eat doggy-do if there was sour cream on it."

Augie tries to suppress the laughter, but he just can't keep his shoulders from shaking. Doggy-do! It's so incredibly stupid.

He wonders if that's how all first-grade teachers say it, or just Mrs. Battle.

Chapter Six

NOW THAT it's warmer, Uncle Emil's back in his ditch again. Every afternoon, as soon as he gets home from the post office, he's digging away. After supper, if it's still light, he gets a little more digging in.

It's a big backyard, fortunately. Otherwise, there'd be no room for anything else but the hole. It's deep, too. More than twenty feet. Augie has to come right up to the edge to see Uncle Emil working down there.

"How much deeper?" Augie asks.

"Till I see the stars," Uncle Emil reminds him.

"You can see stars any night that's clear," Augie reminds him.

"I want to see them in the middle of the day," Uncle Emil says. "Like the Mayans did."

It's true. Uncle Emil showed him the book. It's something Indians in Mexico did. About ten thousand years ago. They figured out you could see the stars during the day if you dug deep enough. It was the only proof they had that the stars didn't go somewhere else when the sun was up.

As soon as Uncle Emil read about it, he started the

ditch. The folks at the post office are always teasing him about it. Augie can't blame them. He'd bet even some Mayans thought it was a little weird.

But Honey says it beats getting drunk, which is what a lot of guys do. (Like it has to be one or the other. Augie never imagines Mr. Bob Wyatt getting drunk or digging a big, dumb hole.)

"But everyone knows the stars are there even if you don't see them," Augie says. "Can't you take their word for it?"

"I got to see them for myself," Uncle Emil says.

Augie walks back toward the house. Just as he is about to open the kitchen door, he turns back to his uncle. "You know the Atlantic Ocean exists," Augie says. "And Mount Everest."

"It's stars I care about," Uncle Emil says.

Chapter Seven

THE KIDS dawdle outside, waiting for the first bell. The girls gossip and giggle in little clusters on the steps. The guys hang out in the parking lot.

"Monkey in the middle!" someone yells.

A lunch box sails through the air. Chris Garelik leaps for it.

"Marty!" Chris shouts as he hurls the lunch box toward Marty Kuhlman. "Catch!"

Blue Tebaldo runs frantically back and forth between Chris and Marty. "Give it back to me, guys," he pleads. "Give it back!"

He leaps into the air, but he's just too short to intercept the flying lunch box.

"Hey, guys!" Kyle shouts. "Why don't you leave the kid alone?"

Next time Marty flings the lunch box into the air, Kyle makes a jump for it. He catches it, but the latch breaks and the lid flips open. Blue's lunch flies out in half a dozen directions. Twinkies, an apple, his Thermos, and a sandwich half out of its Baggie lie all over the asphalt.

"You jerks!" Blue shouts.

Kyle grabs the Twinkies. Denny Swoboda gives Blue back his sandwich. Augie retrieves the Thermos just before it rolls under Mrs. Battle's '96 Stratus. As he hands it to Blue, he sees the tears running down Blue's face.

"What do they want, anyway?" Blue asks.

"You should dye your hair back a regular color," Augie suggests. "No one picked on you when your name was Raymond."

Blue closes the lid on the lunch box. "I like my hair," he says. "I like my new name, too."

"Then you'd better get used to the razzing," Kyle says.

Blue shakes his head. "Get used to that?" he asks. "No way."

"You could buy your lunch," Augie says.

"You ever taste what they sell in the cafeteria?" Blue asks.

"Every day," Augie tells him.

"That stuff is disgusting!"

"Excuse me," Augie says, "but I happen to like disgusting stuff."

The bell rings. The kids start up the front steps.

"And the kids think *I'm* pathetic." Blue sighs as he pushes past Augie into the building.

"We *are* doing nominations before lunch, aren't we?"

With a weary nod, Miss Merkel erases the lists of dominants and recessives from the blackboard. "Anybody you'd like to nominate, Ginger?" she asks.

"Nope," Ginger says.

"Okay," Miss Merkel says. "Anybody feel like nominating anybody?" She picks up some chalk and waits.

"I nominate Marty," Denny says.

No surprise there.

"Second?"

Half the kids second it.

"Anybody else?"

Ginger jabs Augie in the ribs. He grunts in pain.

"Did you say something, Augie?"

"No, Miss Merkel."

"It *sounded* like you," Miss Merkel goes on.

"Oh, yeah," Augie says. "I almost forgot. I nominate Ginger." His throat is so dry, his voice cracks between "nom" and "nate."

He can hear the giggles.

"Second?"

"I second the nomination," Sallie Corn chimes in. Augie wonders how much that set Ginger back.

"I nominate Kyle," says Cupper Marks.

Even if Kyle's his best friend, Augie's surprised when he hears all the "yeahs" and "cools." Kyle didn't used to be so popular.

"Who'll second the nomination?"

"Second!" Everyone's saying it. Except Ginger, probably.

"Anyone else?" Miss Merkel asks as she writes Kyle's name under Ginger's. "Time to vote."

The class puts their heads down on their desks.

"Who's voting for Marty?" Chair legs scrape on the linoleum. Kids are shifting in their seats. Lots of kids are voting for Marty. Augie doesn't need to peek to know that.

"Ginger!"

He takes a peek now. Two, three, four kids ahead of him are voting for Ginger. Sandy. Camille. Lisbeth. Sallie. Why didn't Ginger get Sandy or Camille to nominate her?

"Kyle."

Augie raises his hand. He's got to. Kyle's his best friend. He waits for Miss Merkel to finish the count. He hears the squeak of chalk on blackboard. Everyone can look now.

"Congratulations, Marty."

Heads up now, everyone is clapping.

Marty 12
Ginger 5
Kyle 9

"I saw you, Augie!"

"Saw me?" Augie asks sheepishly.

"How could you vote for someone else after I gave you all that money?" Ginger protests.

"What did you say?" Miss Merkel asks, stepping toward the back of the room.

"I paid Augie," Ginger groans.

"For the nomination," Augie explains. "I never said I'd vote for her, too."

The kids start to laugh.

"How much did you get, Augie?" Benno asks.

"Oh, not all that much," Augie mumbles.

"I gave you ten dollars!" Ginger exclaims.

"You would have lost, anyway," Augie says, "even if I'd voted for you."

Augie hears the kids gasp. Then Benno Kelly starts to clap. Other kids join in. In no time it seems like half the kids are on their feet, cheering for Augie.

"Somebody ought to teach you about principles, Augie Knapp!" Ginger shouts.

Miss Merkel has to pound her desk half a dozen times before the kids give it a rest.

Chapter Eight

SUPPER IS Swiss steak and baked potatoes and frozen peas. It doesn't taste as good as it smells, but it's the only thing Augie's mom can make from scratch. As Honey dishes out the food, Uncle Emil comes in, still sweating from digging all afternoon. His hands are clean, though. Honey makes him wash before he sits down.

"You get to China yet?" Honey asks him.

It's only the one millionth time she's asked.

"Just about," Uncle Emil says. Which is what he says every time.

"Your principal called," Honey tells Augie.

"Mrs. McCann?"

As though anyone gets more than one.

"Wants to see you tomorrow in her office," Honey says, smiling a little.

"She didn't say anything else?"

"Nothing except she's calling Mrs. Izbicki, too," Honey goes on. "You and your little girlfriend in some kind of trouble?"

"She's not my girlfriend," Augie protests.

"Put some sour cream on your potato, Augie," Honey tells him. "It's how you like it."

"I'd prefer it on doggy-do, if you don't mind," Augie tells her.

Uncle Emil leans across the table and slaps his cheek. Hard, too.

"Hey, it was a joke, is all."

"You don't see me laughing, do you?"

Chapter Nine

MRS. McCANN'S gray hair is in a bun. She wears a brown suit. Black shoes. Her wire-frame glasses are sliding down her nose. She nods, says, "Yes, I see," twice into the phone. The glasses slip another quarter of an inch.

She nods again. "Yes, I see," she says again. The glasses slip again. If she doesn't shove them back up her nose, Augie's going to leap out his chair and fix them for her.

Finally, she hangs up. Peering over the frames, she gives the kids the once-over.

"Who paid whom?" she asks.

"She did," Augie says. With a shrug of his shoulders, he indicates the lump slouched in the next chair. Today Ginger's wearing her black sweats. The Izbickis must be having an occasion, Augie figures. Maybe one of Ginger's uncles is getting paroled.

It's Augie's first time in the principal's office. The desk, the bookshelves, even the floor is piled high with folders and books.

"You admit you paid Augie?" Mrs. McCann asks.

"Ten bucks," she says.

"Speak to me, Ginger," Mrs. McCann says. "Not your navel."

"Huh?"

"Sit up, Ginger." Mrs. McCann drops her glasses on the desk. Leaning back, she rubs her eye. "The amount is immaterial," she says wearily.

"It's not your ten bucks," Ginger complains.

"You should have known better," Mrs. McCann goes on. "It's just plain wrong to buy votes."

"But he didn't," Ginger says. "He voted for Kyle."

"You'll have detention, Ginger," Mrs. McCann says. "For a week."

"Just me?" Ginger asks. "What about him?"

Mrs. McCann looks at Augie. "I'll think of something," she says.

"Wish I had a gimpy hand."

"Ginger!"

"Well, it's why, isn't it?" she says.

"You may leave now, Ginger," Mrs. McCann tells her.

But Ginger is already out in the hall. Augie sits there, waiting for Mrs. McCann to say something. When the bell rings, she still hasn't explained what his punishment is going to be. "You'd better run along to class, Augie," she says finally.

Ginger's right, he figures. Sometimes being a gimp pays off.

The rest of the morning, sixth grade might as well be the math channel. Even after Miss Merkel gives the kids a ten-minute quiz, there's more math. Enough is enough.

Augie's not even pretending to listen anymore. If he

tilts his chair back on the rear legs, he can lean his head against the wall. The trick is to see how far back he can go without the chair slipping out from under him.

There's a fish tank on the only unused desk in the classroom. Augie keeps watching one fish in particular. It's all pink and black stripes, and Augie can't keep his eyes off it.

There's a knock on the classroom door.

Even if every kid in the classroom hears it, Miss Merkel doesn't. She keeps on about quotients and divisors. It's only when the door opens that Miss Merkel notices.

"Miss Merkel?" Mrs. McCann says as she takes a step into the classroom.

Augie detects the sudden frown on Miss Merkel's face. Mrs. McCann is the principal, after all.

The women meet halfway. Mrs. McCann whispers something in Miss Merkel's ear.

"Now?" Miss Merkel asks.

"She's outside," Mrs. McCann explains, but it sounds more like she's apologizing.

Miss Merkel shrugs. "We have a new student in our class, boys and girls," she announces as Mrs. McCann retreats to the hall. "She's just moved to town."

It's a big deal, someone new in the class. Hardly anyone ever moves here, Augie thinks.

"Where's she going to sit?" Wendy Kim asks.

"She can have my seat," Benno announces.

He stands up and pretends he's leaving just as Mrs. McCann fetches the new kid. It's a girl, but she's tall. A little taller than Mrs. McCann, even. Augie can't see her face. The brim on the black straw hat is too wide.

She tilts her head back. As Augie sees the face, he gasps. The chair almost topples over.

It's her! It's that girl! Lydie Rose what's-her-face! The one who stole his wristwatch! What's she think she's doing in sixth grade, anyway?

"Sit here," Miss Merkel says to what's-her-face-enheimer, indicating the chair next to the desk with the aquarium on it. "Then I'll introduce everyone to you."

"I already know one person," the girl says playfully.

"Who's that?" Miss Merkel asks Lydie Rose.

It's a struggle for Augie just to get his own chair back on all four legs again. He'd like nothing more than to stick his head into his desk, but it's too late.

"Surprised, Gray?" she asks happily as she points straight at Augie.

The chair slides out from under him. Augie tumbles to the floor. As he lies on the linoleum, the class bursts into major applause.

But he knows what happened to the letter to Gray Dmytryck. What's-her-face-enheimer stole it!

Augie hears the footsteps pound the linoleum behind him.

"Hey, wait up, Gray!"

He keeps walking. The footsteps bear down on him, but he doesn't stop until he feels the hand clasp his shoulder.

"You got cotton candy in your ears or something?" she asks. "Didn't you hear me, Gray?"

"Hey, my name isn't—"

Ignoring him, she scrounges about in her quilted bag. "I tried to give it back," she says as she pulls out the envelope. "I even went to 148 Chestnut Street, but this lady said *she* was Gray Dmytryck. Why would some old woman pretend to be you, Gray?"

Augie snaps the letter from her. "It's her name," he explains.

"You mean there're two people by that name in this dumb little town?" Lydie Rose asks.

"Just one." He sighs. "My name's Augie Knapp."

He tucks the letter in his pocket. Then he resumes walking in the direction he was going before he was so rudely interrupted.

"Gym's the other way," Lydie Rose says, catching up with him.

"I don't go to gym," he says.

"You got a cold?"

Shaking his head, Augie holds up his hand with the glove on it. If anything is going to shut her up, that should do it.

"You still got that cold hand?" Lydie Rose asks. "Is that it?"

He should have known! Nothing shuts this one up. With his other hand, he pushes open the door to the faculty lounge. "You're not allowed here," he tells her.

She follows him inside, anyway.

"You got to go to gym," he tells her.

"If I get me one of those gloves, will they let me out of gym, too?"

Mrs. McCann's secretary has left a pile of papers beside the copier. Next week's menu. The field trips planned for the rest of the year. Augie turns on the copier. "If I just ignore you, will you go away?" he asks.

"Never worked so far," Lydie says cheerfully. She

wanders around the faculty lounge, studying the schedules and posters on the bulletin boards, checking the coin return on the Coke machine for loose change.

As she plops down on the couch, the black straw hat slips off her head. Her hair is extremely curly. No wonder she wears the hat. "You want to go out riding after school?"

"Like you got a car," he mumbles as he tries to read about the trip Miss Novak's fourth grade is taking to the flood museum in Johnstown.

"I know how to drive," she assures him. "Stick shift, too."

"You have to be sixteen," he tells her.

"Bet no one would stop me. You like convertibles, Gray?"

"Augie."

"Oh, right. You like—?"

"I'd like you to get out of here," he says.

As she jumps to her feet, she spots the wastebasket in the corner, brimming over with crumpled-up paper. "Wonder what's in there!" she asks.

"Get out of here, Lydie Rose."

"I know you're dying to." She beams.

"You don't know the first thing about me," Augie insists.

She starts for the door. Finally. She grabs the doorknob and gives it a pull. "I know something else about you, Gray," Lydie Rose says.

"Augie," he says. "It's Augie."

"You're waiting, too," she says. "I knew it the moment I clapped my eyes on you, Gray."

"Waiting for *what*?"

"For the Gypsies to come!" she exclaims.

"What do I want Gypsies for!" he groans.

"Oh, folks like us *need* them!" she insists.

"Us?" Augie asks suspiciously. "Like there's something we have in common?"

"There's no law says you *got* to wear a glove to be special," Lydie insists.

"I'm not special," Augie says.

"Oh, come on!" she protests.

"You get out of here," he tells her.

"You'll hum a different tune when the Gypsies come for you, Gray!" she says. "Everyone does."

"Augie!" he pleads. "My name's Augie."

Too late. She's already skipping down the hall toward gym.

Chapter Ten

AT 11:30, THE gym turns into the cafeteria. Blue metal tables, plus long blue benches, slide out of the walls. Almost all the boys in Miss Merkel's sixth grade eat together at one table. Almost all the girls eat at another.

Today's dessert is peaches in syrup.

Benno Kelly has just named it "Beethoven's Last Movement." Everybody laughed; Augie, too.

"So where's she from, anyway?" Denny asks.

"Who?" Augie asks.

"That girl," Denny says. "Lydie Rose. Don't you know, Augie?"

"Why ask me?"

"You saw her first, didn't you?"

Augie sees her sitting at the next table. With Ginger and Blue. The Nerd Table. It figures. "She didn't say," he says. "Outer space. Erie. Take your pick."

"I bet she came down from the hills," Denny says. "She could be one of them."

The boys nod. Augie included. He's seen them driving through town on Saturday afternoons. Real loud, and poor as dirt, and they never make their kids go to school. Some folks say there're hundreds of hill folks living in shacks and old mines, from when the coal companies still operated here.

"She looks poor enough," Benno says.

"She talks funny, too," Chris Garelik adds.

"I bet she's got hair growing down her back!" Marty Kuhlman exclaims. The boys groan and laugh at the same time. Everyone knows the stories.

"Why'd she call you 'Gray'?" Benno Kelly asks.

"Beats me," Augie says with a shrug.

He already made a jerk of himself when he fell out of his chair. Once a day is enough.

"She's too tall," Benno Kelly says.

"She's ooooo-gleeee," Chris Garelik adds.

"Better throw her back!" Marty Kuhlman says.

The rest of the boys pound the table with their forks and knives. Marty started talking like that about girls at the end of fifth grade. Augie feels his face getting hot. It's stupid, but what can he do about it?

"Hey, Augie!" Marty roars. "Your face is all red."

The boys roar with laughter and pound the table some more. Augie sees the janitor sliding the empty tables back into the wall. The cafeteria is about to turn back into the gym.

When Augie comes back from lunch, it's still early. No one's in the classroom except Denny Swoboda. Denny has a stack of envelopes in his hand.

Standing in the doorway, Augie watches Denny going from desk to desk. When Denny reaches Sal's desk, he drops one of the blue envelopes on it. Greg's desk. Lou's desk. Kyle's desk. Kevin's desk. He's skipping Melanie. And Diane. And Nancy. No girls.

Augie gets it. It's a boy party.

Denny has only one invitation left. When he reaches the back corner, Denny checks the envelope. Well, of course, he's going to drop it on Augie's desk. You don't invite Kyle to something without inviting Augie, too.

Augie steps forward. "Looks like someone's having a party," he says, playfully grabbing for the envelope.

"You scared me, Augie!" Denny exclaims. He tries to grab the envelope back, but Augie's already looking at the name on it.

Oh, no! The envelope's got Eddie's name on it!

"It's for the guys in Little League," Denny says. "This year, you know."

"Oh, sure," Augie says, handing the envelope back to Denny.

"It's not like the guys don't like you," Denny stammers. "It's just you don't play."

Augie grins. "Well, I might," he says.

"Huh?"

"I got my own mitt, don't I?"

Denny shakes his head.

Augie waves the glove at him. "My mitt?" he says. "Get it now?"

Denny smiles, finally. "I get it," he says. "That's pretty funny, Augie."

"You know how I always kid around," Augie says.

"Just as long as you don't feel like you got left out," Denny says.

The green blazer on top belongs to Shelby deForest.

It's all she wears, practically. The Kleenex goes in the trash. The comb goes into a plastic Baggie that he safety-pins to the lining.

He finds a bracelet. Gold, too. That goes in the plastic bag. In the last pocket he finds three nickels and some pennies. Mrs. Lumaghi says anything under a buck he gets to keep.

He moves onto Junior Gertz's blue suit. Right away he strikes pay dirt in the inside breast pocket. Two condoms. In a blue foil. With "lubrication."

Augie crams Junior Gertz's former condoms into his pocket, along with Shelby deForest's former change. He can't imagine Junior Gertz asking Mrs. Lumaghi for his condoms back.

When he gets home from Mrs. Lumaghi's, he calls up Kyle. But Kyle's still at Little League practice. So Augie spends the rest of the afternoon in the barn.

Counting what he just confiscated from Junior Gertz, Augie's now got nine condoms. Seven different brands. Some "with lube." Some without. Marty Kuhlman would bust a gut if he found out Augie Knapp has the most extensive condom collection of any sixth grader in Warsaw Junction.

Augie checks the envelope Lydie returned to him in the faculty lounge. Gray Dmytryck's name and the address are so smudged now, he can hardly read them. He doesn't bother trying.

As soon as he picks up the Christmas card, he starts pretending he's a Wyatt. Doesn't matter which one. Wyatts always get invited to everyone's birthday party.

Even the dog.

Chapter Eleven

AUGIE LEANS against the jungle gym, chewing a blade of the new batch of grass that's been greening up. Blue's perched on top of the jungle gym, drawing something in his sketchbook. All the other boys are tossing a football around.

The girls are sitting on the grass. Except Ginger. She never did show up for school that day.

"What's the best grade?" Nancy Socci asks.

"Second," announces Cupper Marks. "Because they closed the school for two weeks on account of the Asian flu."

"Third because of Mrs. Bladen's fish," Sallie Corn decides.

"Kindergarten!" Billie says. She doesn't explain, and no one asks. But everyone laughs just the same.

"Tenth grade," Zina Bowhan announces.

"You haven't been to tenth grade yet!" Melanie protests.

"Well, it's got to be best," Zina insists. "It's when you get your driver's license."

"What's your favorite grade, Lydie Rose?" Melanie asks.

"Oh, sixth is always nice."

"Always?" Melanie asks, a little suspicious. "How many sixth grades you been to?"

"Well, they're all over these days," Lydie assures the kids. "Anytime you feel like a little sixth grade, there's bound to be one handy."

The girls giggle.

"How old are you, Lydie?" Zina asks.

"How old do you think?" Lydie asks.

"Older than us," Zina says cautiously.

"When you guys get so serious, I feel I'm a lot younger," Lydie says.

"They want to know what age you are, Lydie," Augie says. "Why not tell them?"

"When you come right down to it, age is more like an attitude," Lydie says.

"That's it?" Augie asks.

"That's it!"

If the kids didn't know how peculiar Lydie Rose was before, they do now.

Chapter Twelve

IT'S GETTING warmer. The earth smells fill the air.

People leave their windows open now. As Augie delivers the laundry, he hears things. The TV. Dishes, too. You don't think of dishes as being noisy, but they are if it's mealtime.

The birds are back. Over the weekend, finches have settled into the birdhouse Augie made in fourth grade. When Augie rides the trike home, he hears them singing.

He sees the water rushing through the big pipe under Hannah Avenue. He jumps off the trike and races across the yard, past the barn. It's melted. Finally! The stream down the mountain is flowing again. It's alive again.

He heads next door to the Warnkes'.

Kyle's dad is outside, putting up a new mailbox. It's dark blue, and it has a bird on it, plus 415 HANNAH on the side. The bird is red, which means it's probably a cardinal.

"How about that, Augie?"

"It's nice, Mr. Warnke," Augie says. "Is Kyle around?"

"No one's home, Augie," he shouts. "Kyle just left five

minutes ago. If you run, you can catch up with him."

"Where's that, Mr. Warnke?"

"Denny's," Mr. Warnke says as he gets into the pickup. "How come you're not there? It's his birthday."

"I guess I forgot," Augie says.

"If you want, I can give you a lift. You don't want to miss the ice cream and cake."

"It's okay, Mr. Warnke," he says. "I'll walk."

He watches Mr. Warnke pull out of the driveway. Augie spots something in the grass. It's a baseball bat. He bends down and picks it up.

He's seen batters a million times. Not just Little Leaguers. But the guys on television. All you do is plant your legs firmly on the ground like this, wrap both hands around the bat, and wait for the ball.

He grips the bat in his right hand. Standing in the middle of the Warnkes' front yard, he waves the bat at an imaginary ball. If he connected—and he probably wouldn't, since he hasn't got any leverage with only one hand—the best he'd get would be a bunt.

The street's quiet. No one's out. It's like the whole world got invited to Denny's birthday party. Not that he's sore. What would he be doing at a Little League party, anyway? He plants his legs on the ground. Augie raises the Major League bat as high as he can. With all his might, he slams it down hard on the Warnkes' new mailbox.

The big red bird now has a Major League dent in it.

Chapter Thirteen

LYDIE ARRIVES at school, clasping a basket of daffodils. Augie sees her beaming and bowing to the kids like she was just elected queen of sixth grade. When the bell rings, everyone rushes inside.

He follows her down the hall to the water fountain. It's the only water fountain in the whole Warsaw Junction public school system that works. But instead of sticking her mouth into the water, she sticks the basket under it.

"Got to keep my daffies in water or they won't last," Lydie says.

"But the water will leak out," Cupper warns her.

"Don't you worry," Lydie Rose exclaims. She holds the basket over her head. No water seeps through.

The kids gasp.

"Is that something the Gypsies could teach me to do, Lydie Rose?" Augie asks.

Lydie looks at him. Smiles. She walks toward him and sticks her face in his. "There's plenty of things the Gypsies are going to teach you, Augie Knapp," she whispers.

"You still think they're coming for me?" Augie laughs.

"They're on their way," Lydie tells him. "You don't have much waiting time left."

Miss Merkel has just this minute assigned term papers. First time ever. She says they need to be prepared for junior high school in the fall.

"It's a map," Miss Merkel explains, "of your genes."

"But a map tells you where you're going," Lydie Rose says.

(Even though Miss Merkel offered to put the aquarium somewhere else, Lydie insisted it stay right on her desk.)

"Except this one tells you where you come from," Miss Merkel says. "It tells you where you got your red hair, Lydie. Or where Denny gets his curly hair."

"Everyone in my family has curly hair," Denny says.

"How about your eyes? Does everyone in your family have brown eyes?"

"No," Denny says. "My dad's got blue eyes."

"What if you have blue hair?" Lydie asks.

"No one—"

"Blue does!" Lydie says.

"Well, that's out of a bottle," Miss Merkel says. "That's not out of Blue's gene pool."

"I've got blue jeans," Benno says, laughing, jumping out of his seat. "I'm wearing mine."

"But what if someone had blue hair?" Kevin Costello asks. "And it didn't come from a bottle?"

"Then it's what they call a mutation," Miss Merkel says. "It's a genetic accident."

"Blue's a mutant!" Benno laughs. "He's the mutant from the blue lagoon!"

Augie expects Blue to make a big deal of it. But Blue's laughing his head off along with the rest of them.

The clothes are piled, as usual, in the corner. Augie starts going through the pockets. Today it's all Kleenex and candy wrappers and pennies and paper clips.

He's almost to the bottom of the pile when he finds a letter. It's in the pocket of the ugliest sweater he ever saw. The envelope is all wrinkled, too. Making sure the coast is clear, he opens the envelope and slips out the letter inside.

~~Gray~~
Augie,

When the heck are you going to stop going through other people's stuff?

Love ya,
Lydie Rose

Chapter Fourteen

HONEY'S OLDSMOBILE is parked in the driveway. The trunk is open. It's filled with shopping bags.

"Augie?"

"I see them, Mom!"

Cradling two of them in his arms, he staggers up the back steps.

Honey is at the sink, peeling brown things. "Your little girlfriend left something for you," Honey says.

Augie drops the bags on the kitchen table. He sees the envelope on the lazy Susan. "That's it?" he asks.

"Maybe it's a love letter," Honey says.

"You think so?"

"Bet you a dollar," Honey says.

Augie rips open the envelope. Inside is a piece of lined school paper with two holes in the side.

Dear Augie,

When my brothers beat you up, you'll know what sorry is.

Sincerely,

Ginger

"You owe me a buck," he says, cramming the letter in his pocket.

"You and Ginger aren't boyfriend and girlfriend anymore?"

"Kind of looks that way," he says.

A car pulls up to the house. It's a late-model Volvo. A man gets out. It's Mr. Krulis. From Krulis-Hallmark. He's got his suit on, too.

Augie's seen him around lots of times. His wife and his son got killed in a car accident last year. So you can't help feeling for him, even if you don't know what you're supposed to say to someone like that.

Still lingering behind the azaleas, Augie watches him walk up toward the house. He's tall, probably six feet. He's got a crew cut that's going gray. Prematurely. He can't be more than mid-thirties. Plus, he's thin. Compared with the guys Honey knows down at the beer factory, this guy's a beanpole.

"Hi, there, Augie," Mr. Krulis says.

"Hi."

"How's it going?"

"Okay."

"Bet you can't wait for summer."

"Yeah."

"That's how it was when I was a kid. Your mom home?"

"I guess."

"Well, nice talking to you, Augie," he says.

"Okay," Augie says.

Mr. Krulis walks up the front steps and rings the bell. Augie dashes around back.

"What's Mr. Krulis want with Mom?" Augie asks Uncle Emil.

"He's taking her to a movie."

"You mean it's like a date?"

"You figure," Uncle Emil says.

"Does she like him?"

"She hangs out at the card shop enough," Uncle Emil says.

"I thought she just liked the cards," Augie says.

"Life's just chock full of surprises, huh, Augie?"

Augie stands at his window staring out at the night. The Warnkes' TV is up too loud again on account of Kyle's grandmother. Edna Mae is running off at the mouth about the mess Lou left for her in the basement. Sounds like Rocco, the Hamblins' cat, is in another fight in the alley.

A car slows down. The streetlamp's not bright enough for him to tell what kind of car, but he guesses it's Mr. Krulis bringing Honey home.

But the car doesn't stop. As it picks up speed again, it backfires three times. It's no late-model Volvo. It's just someone's wreck. Augie figures Honey and Mr. Krulis must have gone to a long movie.

Someone over at the Warnkes' turns the TV down. All Augie hears are creepers. He never heard them so loud before. There must be a million of them out there tonight.

The Izbicki brothers could be out there, too. For all he knows, they could be staring at Augie's window right this minute. He wishes Mr. Krulis would come back right now.

Chapter Fifteen

IN HIS DREAM they are sitting at a long table. Men, mostly, but there's a woman. She's fat. Not too young. Not too pretty. Her skin is so white, it doesn't really look like flesh at all. In her black hair is a rose. She wears a green dress. The fringe around her waist is as red as the rose, as red as her lips. As one of the men strums a guitar, the woman rises. Slowly, heavily, she begins to dance by herself. Another man shakes a tambourine above his head. The others rap the tabletop with their knuckles to a slow, hard beat.

The rhythm picks up. The woman dances around the table, faster now, lighter. Her face begins to lose its fierceness. She cocks her head. It's as though she is listening for something. Augie listens, too.

"What's happening?" Augie asks the woman.

The woman puts her fingers to her lips, gesturing Augie to be silent. As she listens, he hears it, too. At first it sounds like a machine gun going off somewhere beyond the shadows.

"It's him," the woman says.

Augie listens. He hears the heels of the boots clicking to the beat of the music.

"They're coming," the woman tells him.

"Who?"

"You know," she says.

"I don't!" he protests.

The woman smiles as the clicking gets louder, closer.

How could anyone sleep through that racket?

He wakes up. The music from the guitars and tambourines dies abruptly.

Wide awake, though, he still hears the heels clicking against the tile floor.

Chapter Sixteen

AS AUGIE passes Lydie Rose's desk, he checks out the daffodils. Inside the wicker basket is a Maxwell House coffee can.

That's how come the water doesn't leak through the wicker! Some Gypsy trick!

"You want your money back?" Augie asks her just before the bell.

Ginger takes the money without comment.

"Are we even now?" he asks.

"I'm still doing detention," she reminds him as she crams the bill into the pocket of her sweats. "That sound fair to you?"

Mrs. Jonas comes in for her plaid skirt, but Augie can't find it. He runs the rack around three times before he finally gives up. "Mrs. Lumaghi!" he shouts.

The television is so loud, she can't hear him.

"There's someone can't find her skirt," he says when

he goes to the back of the store. "I ran the rack around three times."

She nods, but doesn't move from her chair.

"Mrs. Lumaghi, there's a—"

"It's DNA Tuesday," she mumbles impatiently, not taking her eyes off the television.

As Augie turns toward the set, he sees Montel and some kid, a guy not more than twenty, nervously wiping the sweat from his forehead.

"Is he or is he not father of baby Timmy Ray?" Montel asks the studio audience and all the folks at home. "May we have the DNA results now, Dr. Prosnick?"

A woman in the first row stands up. She's wearing a white lab coat.

"That's the doc," Mrs. Lumaghi says excitedly. "She used to do DNA for Sally Jessy."

Augie looks back to the TV screen.

"Well, is Gurney baby Timmy Ray's dad?" Montel asks Dr. Prosnick.

Gurney flashes a nervous smile.

"Ninety-nine point sixty-three out of a hundred chances he is," Dr. Prosnick announces.

The audience bursts into loud cheers. Mrs. Lumaghi clicks her tongue. The camera zooms back to Gurney.

A teenage girl, her hair in rollers, is placing a screaming infant into Gurney's arms.

"So how do you feel, Gurney?" Montel asks.

The kid holds the baby in the air like it had cooties. "Me, a dad?" he asks. As Gurney rolls his eyes, he bursts into big, stupid laughter. "It's just too (bleep)ing weird!"

"That's for sure," Mrs. Lumaghi agrees as she shuts off the television.

He's got two suits and a raincoat left. As he pedals the trike down Dogwood Lane, he remembers what he heard about Ms. Conger pretending to take that cruise in the Caribbean last winter and all the time she was hiding out in her own house with the lights off.

At #39, the Schafers have a statue of Mary that's as big as real life. But since the statue's on the front lawn, it's not technically a secret. It's just weird.

Mrs. Smedlow is home, so Augie leaves the raincoat. No one's at the Brownings', but Augie leaves the suits with their next-door neighbor.

As he starts down Fourth Street, he notices the big yellow house. #31. Gus Wiltz is overdrawn at the First Bank of Warsaw. He knows about all the parking tickets Flora Wolfe at #41 has outstanding.

Okay, so it's not like someone's buried in the cellar. Or has three breasts like that lady on the front page of *The Tattler.* But it beats thinking about the Little League opener next week or the flyers for the Beavers' Father-Son Banquet that are tacked to half the telephone poles in town.

The cage rattles as he turns onto Hannah Avenue. Three more blocks till he's home. But it's uphill, and the pedaling is harder.

"Hey, gimp! We got a little business . . ."

He looks over his shoulder, mostly to see who they're yelling at. It's two guys in black leather jackets. They're running down the middle of the street, waving their hands in the air.

Augie flinches as he recognizes those mean faces with their mean, squinty eyes.

It's Ginger's brothers!

Chapter Seventeen

AUGIE SLAMS his feet down on the pedals. When he reaches the corner, he doesn't even slow down. Without looking left or right, he pedals the trike across the intersection.

He hears their boots pounding down the sidewalk. He doesn't have to look back to know they're gaining on him.

"Hey, gimp!"

Louder now.

Augie's trying to pedal harder, but he's already exhausted. No wonder you never see trikes in action movies. They're not built for speed.

"We got you, Augie boy!"

Ralph grabs the front fender. As he raises the front end of the bike a good two feet into the air, Augie keeps pedaling. The wheel spins around furiously, but Augie's not going anywhere.

From behind, Dave grabs Augie under his armpits and starts dragging him off his seat.

"Get your hands off me!" Augie screams. He kicks

frantically at them, but only manages to send the trike toppling over on its side.

"Somebody!" Augie shrieks. "Somebody!"

The neighborhood is deserted. Ralph and Dave drag him into the empty lot across the street. They fling him into the bushes. The briars pierce his shirt. He feels them tearing away at his skin.

Dave pins Augie's arms to the ground. The b.o. is enough to make Augie want to puke. The other one, Ralph, straddles Augie. The same fat, greasy face as Dave. Black hair, cut short like a marine.

"You know what a pink belly is?" Ralph asks. His breath is like he ate a septic tank for lunch.

Augie can't speak. All he does is shake his head violently back and forth.

Ralph rips Augie's shirt down the middle, tearing the buttons from the cloth. "I guess I'll have to show you," he says, slapping Augie's stomach with his right hand.

"Ah!" Augie gasps softly, involuntarily.

Ralph hears it. He smiles. Then he slaps him with his left hand. Right hand. Left hand. Right hand. Left hand. Augie tries to hold it in, but the pain gets more intense. With each slap, it's more like a knife cutting his stomach. Augie groans out loud now.

Left hand.

Right hand.

Left hand.

The skin on his stomach feels so raw. If he can just keep from crying, just keep from crying, just keep from crying, just keep from crying. . . .

Bam!

It's a car backfiring.

Ralph doesn't look up. Maybe he didn't hear.

Augie hears a door slam. Footsteps stomp across the gravel toward them.

"You cretins get the hell out of here!"

Oh, no! How did she . . . ?

"You lay off!" Lydie Rose screams.

"Go away, girlie," Ralph says. "We're teaching the kid a little lesson."

"You couldn't teach someone how to wipe their nose!" Lydie Rose shouts.

Ralph jumps to his feet. "You'd better watch that mouth of yours," he shouts as he steps menacingly toward her.

Lydie steps back. Augie sees the fear on her face. She bends over for something. It's a lead pipe. As Ralph takes another step toward her, she brings the pipe down on him.

Just in time, he rolls out of the way.

Dave crawls up behind her. He's about to grab her ankles, pull her off her feet. Augie tries to warn her but he's gasping so hard, he can barely speak.

She goes into a wild dance, stomping around in a circle like a crazy lady. Dave makes another grab for her ankles, but she kicks him in the face.

"You'll regret that big time, girlie," Ralph yells.

Lydie swings the pipe at him again. He grabs the other end. He tries to pull the pipe away from her, but she won't let go.

Augie sees Lydie tilt her head to the sky. She closes her eyes. Is she giving up, he wonders?

"Aaaaaaaaaaah!"

It starts low, like a moan. It rises, higher and higher.

It's an awful, animal screech. Even the wild coyotes on the ridges can't make noises like that.

"Aaaaaaaaaaaah!"

The louder she chants, the bigger, the fiercer she grows. With a ferocious tug, Lydie pulls the pipe away from Ralph. Grasping it tightly, she swings it at his groin.

"You're crazy!" he groans, dropping to his knees.

"Don't you ever go picking on my friends ever again," Lydie shrieks.

The Izbicki brothers stagger toward the street. Waving the pipe in the air, she chases them all the way. It's not until they're out of sight that Lydie tosses the pipe into the brush.

Augie rolls over in the weeds, clutching his side. His stomach feels like it's on fire, too tender to touch. "How'd you know?"

"I seen your trike lying on its side in the street," she explains.

She waits until he gets his breath back. She helps him with his shirt. Just the touch of the fabric on his raw skin makes him wince with pain. Taking him by the arm, she leads him out of the lot.

"I got me a convertible now," Lydie says proudly. "Just like I said I would."

"Where?" Augie asks.

"There!" she exclaims, pointing toward the street.

It looks to Augie more like the sum total of every rusting wreck he ever saw. Maybe once it was a sedan, maybe even a station wagon. But it's got no top. So it's a convertible, technically.

His trike lies on its side a few feet away. It takes Lydie

only a minute to rope it to the back of her car. "I figure you could use a lift," she says.

"You could get arrested for driving without a license," he tells her.

"What makes you so sure I don't have a license?" she asks.

For once, Augie doesn't protest. When Lydie holds the passenger door open for him, he gets in.

As soon as she starts up the engine, it backfires. The car doesn't go faster than ten miles an hour, and it farts all the way.

"You turn left at the next block," he tells her.

"Yeah, I know," she tells him.

"How?"

But she doesn't reply, and he's hurting too much to press. As they pass the Warnkes' house, he sinks a little in his seat. He doesn't need Kyle to see him like this.

But when they pull up in front of his house, he lets her open the passenger door for him. She unties the trike and sets it down at the foot of Augie's driveway.

"I guess I'm supposed to thank you," he tells her.

"Hey, you and me got to stick together, Augie," Lydie Rose tells him. "We're birds of a feather, if you know what I mean."

"Oh, that again!" Augie groans.

"It's okay," Lydie continues. "I can take it. I *am* a little different. Look at my clothes! You ever notice the way I talk? We're in the same boat, Augie."

Augie shakes his head. "I don't talk funny. I wear the exact same clothes as everyone else. I live in a regular house, too."

"You know what I'm talking about, Augie," Lydie Rose

declares. "Even if you didn't wear that funny little glove all the time, you'd be weird. It's just the way we are."

Augie grabs the handlebar of his trike and starts walking the trike up the driveway.

"Next time the Izbicki brothers beat me up, do me a favor, Lydie Rose," he says without looking back.

"What's that, Augie?"

"Mind your own business," he says.

Chapter Eighteen

HE NOTICES Honey's new cards on the counter. He sifts through them. More cards for more occasions.

When's Hallmark coming out with a card for *his* occasion?

Hope you had fun
with the
Izbicki brothers, Augie.

Turn the cover:

Call us as soon as
you're out
of intensive care!

If he sits still, it doesn't hurt too much. The Vaseline helps, even if Lydie Rose did recommend it. But he didn't tell Honey about it. Or Uncle Emil. What could they do, except make him feel worse about it?

He stares at the computer screen. He's working on the genetics assignment.

Well, his black hair and his brown eyes have to come

from somewhere, and they didn't come from Honey. What else has he got that didn't come from her?

Augie holds the glove up to his nose and takes a whiff. Honey tells him to wash it out before bed and it'll be dry in the morning. If you don't wash it, it gets to smelling, but most of the time, he forgets.

"Augie?"

Augie goes to the window. In the moonlight, he can see Kyle standing on the lawn. "What's up?"

"You want to come out?"

"Now?"

"We could go up the mountain, find out where the stream starts," he suggests.

"How we going to see this time of night?"

"There's the moon," Kyle says. "It'll be okay."

"I'm doing my gene map," Augie tells him.

"It's not due till next week," Kyle reminds him.

Augie leans forward on the sill. The pain in his stomach hits him all over again. "I want to start it early."

Kyle walks across the lawn. Just as he is about to disappear into the night, he turns. "How do you do a gene map if you don't know what your dad looked like?" he asks.

Augie shrugs and closes the window.

Chapter Nineteen

WHAT WOKE him?

He sits up suddenly in his bed. Moonlight shines through the water-stained window so bright, he shields his eyes. Can moonlight wake someone up? he wonders.

From his window he surveys the night. As the wind blows through the trees, shadows dance across Hannah Avenue. He should go back to bed, but he can't sleep now. One slipper's under the bed. The other's on the bureau. He has to walk gingerly. It's an old house. Honey's room is next to his. Uncle Emil's is across the hall. One squeak and one of them will be sending him back to bed.

He creeps sideways down the stairs. When he reaches the landing, he darts across the hall to the dining room. Pausing a moment, he sees the moonlight on the mahogany credenza. He slips into the kitchen and peers out the window over the sink. Is that a light on in the barn? Can't be. Just the moonlight playing tricks on the glass. But he's got to check it out . . . just in case.

The down parka is on a hook in the mudroom. It takes a moment to unlock the back door. He creeps across the backyard, grass crunching under his slippers. He opens the barn door and steps cautiously inside.

Listens.

Nothing.

Finally, he tiptoes through the barn till he comes to the last stall. With his good hand, Augie gropes the wall. The key. He can't find it. Did it fall off the nail?

Anxious, he falls to his knees. Pushes away the hay. Where's the suitcase? It's got to be here. Pushes away more hay. Got to be. Got to be.

Augie feels dizzy, like someone punched the air out of him. Rocking back and forth on his knees, he digs deeper and deeper into the hay. How could it disappear? No one knows about it. It's his secret.

It's *got* to be here.

Chapter Twenty

TODAY AT recess, the dog is hanging around the swings. As soon as Lydie comes out on the playground, it starts wagging its big brown mangy tail.

"How long you had that dog, Lydie?" Cupper asks.

"It's not mine," Lydie says.

As the dog waddles up to her, the girls step back. You can't blame them. It's the smell. Like it just this minute got out of a pond.

"How come it follows you around?" E. Banacek says. "You feed it?"

"If I got anything left over at home," Lydie says.

"You let it stay in your house?"

"Well, it's got to sleep somewhere, don't it?"

Augie sits on the jungle gym. He sees the other girls exchanging secret glances. Lydie continues patting the dog, like she doesn't even notice.

"Where's that?" Zina says.

"Not so far," Lydie says.

"Are your people here, Lydie?" Melanie asks.

"People?" Lydie asks.

"Family," Melanie explains. "You know, your mom and your dad. Don't you have any sisters and brothers?"

Lydie shakes her head. "I got no people here."

"Are they back in the hills?"

"Could be," she says.

"Is that where you're from?" Melanie asks.

"How do you expect me to answer all these questions when my dog is sick!" Lydie exclaims.

"That dog's just a stray!" Augie tells her. "And it's not sick, either!"

As if on cue, Dog starts to whimper. Frantically, it starts limping around like it really is hurt.

"Anyone know a vet around here?" Lydie asks.

As soon as he gets home, he checks the barn. The suitcase still isn't there. What if it was the Izbicki brothers? What are they going to do now?

Probably, if they'd finished beating him up, his suitcase would be in the barn right now. "That Lydie!" he exclaims angrily.

The house smells funny. As soon as he comes in the back door, he notices it. She's painting again. Upstairs, the hall is crammed with furniture. Honey's on a stepladder in her room, painting her ceiling.

"What do you call this one?" he asks as he leans against the door frame.

Honey steps down the ladder and sticks the roller in the pan. "Mountain Reverie," she tells him. "Trish picked it out."

"It looks like blue to me," he says.

"You know Harv Krulis thinks you're quite a kid?"

"He said so?"

Honey nods, wiping a smudge of Mountain Reverie from her cheek. "You like him, Augie?"

"He drives a Volvo," Augie replies.

"What's that supposed to mean?" Honey asks.

Augie shrugs. If Honey were in sixth grade, she wouldn't have to ask. "What's it matter what I think?" Augie asks.

"He likes you, Augie."

"He tell you that?"

Honey nods as she picks up the roller again.

"He doesn't know me," Augie says.

"He sees you riding Mrs. Lumaghi's trike," Honey says. "He says you and him had a nice talk the other day."

Stepping up her ladder, she rolls out another stroke of Mountain Reverie on her ceiling.

"How old was his kid that died?" Augie asks.

"Sixteen," Honey says.

"Does he miss him?"

"What kind of man wouldn't feel horrible about that?"

Shrugging, Augie starts down the hall. When he reaches the top of the stairs, he turns and walks back. "Does my own dad know about me?"

Honey nods so cautiously, it's almost imperceptible.

"Did he see *this,* Mom?" he asks as he raises his gloved hand to his face. "Did he see my hand?"

"Your hand didn't have anything to do with it," she tells him.

"It's got to be the hand," Augie mutters.

"Oh, Augie, what difference does it make?" Honey asks. "He's gone, is all. You're just going to get yourself all upset."

"Right," Augie says.

He doesn't need to get upset. He's going to the barn to see how the Wyatts are doing. He's halfway there before he remembers someone's stolen his suitcase.

Now the Wyatts are gone, too.

Chapter Twenty-One

WHEN HE comes up the Warnkes' front steps the next morning, he hears Mr. Warnke inside shouting. Probably at Kyle's big brother, Ulee.

Mrs. Warnke opens the storm door and sticks her head out on the porch. She's a nervous little woman, given to smiling and fidgeting, usually at the same time. "Kyle's running late this morning," she says.

"I'm early."

"I'd invite you inside, but—"

"I can wait out here," Augie says.

As he perches on the railing, Mrs. Warnke smiles and goes back inside. Even with the door closed, he can hear every word.

"You show a little respect for a change," Mr. Warnke shouts. "If I say you're going somewhere, you're getting over there."

"Make Ulee go!"

"You know why I don't take Ulee. You'd think maybe I'd get one kid who doesn't treat me like a bad smell."

The door swings open. Kyle bursts out onto the

porch. He's mad, too. He slams the storm door so hard, the glass almost shatters. "You're lucky you don't have to put up with that stuff," he groans as he stomps down the stairs.

Kyle's pounding the pavement so furiously that Augie has to run to keep up. It's not till they reach the corner of Fifth and Chestnut that Kyle looks semi-sane again.

"Where's he want you to go?" Augie asks.

"It's the Beavers," Kyle tells him. "Their annual banquet. They drink and they tell dumb jokes and they make you wear their dumb Beaver pins."

"What he's need you there for?"

"It's their father-and-son evening," Kyle explains. "You got to bring a kid or they won't let you in."

Augie starts to laugh.

"What's so funny?"

"Oh, nothing," Augie says. "I'm just glad I got no one making me go."

"You got time for a drop-off?" Mrs. Lumaghi asks.

Augie shrugs. "How far?"

"Ash Street, " she says. "A couple of suits. They'll give you a tip if you get there in an hour."

He looks at the receipt. "Joe Blow?" he asks. "That's supposed to be a real name?"

Mrs. Lumaghi shrugs. "You got an address," she tells him. "That's all you need."

"No one's named Joe Blow," Augie insists.

"Check the receipt, then."

Well, it could be "Blow." But the handwriting's so messy, it could be some other names, too. As Augie pedals the trike across town, he's got to wonder why someone would take their clothes to Mrs. Lumaghi when Minnie's Martinizing is right around the corner.

But it's still not five yet, and Augie's got nothing better to do than earn a couple of extra bucks.

He turns onto Ash. 47, 45, 43.

Most of the houses have the names right on the mailbox. He recognizes all of them, too. No mailbox at 41. Probably they haven't got around to putting one up yet.

Augie brings the trike to a stop. He grabs the suits from the back. As he steps toward the house, he can't help noticing that the suits have got to be the crummiest-looking clothes he ever delivered to anyone.

He knocks on the door.

No answer.

He knocks again. "Mr. Blow?" he calls out.

"Come on in," a voice calls back. "Door's not locked."

Slowly, Augie pushes on the door. It creaks open a few inches.

He pushes the door again and steps inside. The living room is a mess. Magazines, newspapers everywhere. The living room's empty, but the TV's on.

"Mr. Blow?" Augie calls again. "I got your dry cleaning. I'm from Mrs. Lumaghi's."

"I'm in the back!" It's a peculiar voice. Mr. Blow sounds like he has a cold.

"I'll just leave the clothes here," Augie shouts. Augie notices a photograph on top of the TV. Three kids. A girl about Augie's age, with her two older brothers.

He knows who's on the other side of that door. It's a trap! He knows what they're planning to do to him, too! What a jerk! He should have suspected something like this all along.

"Come on back if you want your tip."

But he's already halfway across the living room. He doesn't look back. He doesn't have to. He already knows what an Izbicki looks like.

He dashes across the porch and down the steps. Mrs. Lumaghi's trike is on the sidewalk where he left it. That's the last thing he needs. He's got to hide.

Now!

As he tears down the street, he hears the Izbickis' door slam.

Four houses up the block is his best chance. The roof has fallen through, the walls are blistered and scarred, the front porch has fallen off.

The front yard looks like the local dump. A rusted-out washing machine lies on its side in the front yard. Augie dives behind it just as he hears the Izbickis running down the street.

"Where did the little creep go?" Ralph asks.

"Up the street, I guess," Dave says.

"You guess?"

"How am I supposed to know?"

He hears metal clattering onto the asphalt. He's too afraid to peer around the washing machine, but he knows without looking that they've knocked his trike over.

"You'd better go that way," Ralph says. "I'll go toward Seventh. First one finds him drags him back here."

"Then we'll start the party?" Dave asks.

"You got it!"

Augie hears them running along the street in opposite directions. How long is it going to take before they realize he hasn't gone in either direction, he wonders. The grass, still brown from winter, comes to a man's waist. Augie crawls through it, around to the back. Safer there, he knows.

The kitchen steps are broken. He has to be careful. Still kneeling, he raises his head just high enough to look through the window. There's a mattress on the floor. Clothes are piled in the corner.

Squatters, maybe. Or just a bum who spent the night here. How long ago, there's no saying. The kitchen table is covered with all sorts of junk. A jar of Skippy, with the lid off. A scrunched-up bag of chips. A bottle of that French mineral water they advertise on TV. Some old magazines. Bits and pieces of paper.

On top of the cupboard is a suitcase. It's old and brown. It's got water stains all over, too. There must be hundreds of suitcases like that, right in Warsaw Junction, too. But it's his. Augie knows that for sure.

Chapter Twenty-Two

THERE'S NO lock on the door. Not even a doorknob. But whoever it is could be upstairs, or even in the next room. It could be a drunk. Or some nut.

Augie gives the door a push. Even an alcoholic lunatic can't be more dangerous than the Izbicki brothers. Cautiously, he steps inside.

A gust of wind comes up. As the door slams shut, Augie jumps. He holds his breath till everything is still again. He stares at the papers on the table. He recognizes the pink slip Miss Merkel's sister got from the phone company. Next to it is Benno Kelly's report card.

Standing on his tiptoes, he can almost reach the suitcase on top of the cupboard. He needs something to stand on. There's a chair by the door. It's creaky, but it should do. He sets it by the cupboard and steps up on it. So far, so good. He reaches for the suitcase. Looks inside, but only for a second. No time to dawdle. Hugging the suitcase tight, he jumps off the chair.

As he hits the floor, he doesn't stop. A rotted floorboard gives way, and Augie's left leg falls through the hole. His arms flail about as he struggles for balance; the suitcase tumbles out of his arms. Augie sees it burst open in midair, spilling papers everywhere.

His behind crashes to the floor. One leg is stretched out in front of him, the other is in the hole. When he pushes the board away, it snaps back, trapping him.

Gasping for breath, he barely hears the car farting to a stop. He doesn't hear the footsteps rustling the grass. He doesn't hear the door creak open.

"Well, I guess I should feel flattered you dropped in," she says.

(Well, of course. Who else? And just when he figured it couldn't get any worse.)

Laughing at her own joke, Lydie Rose drops her two A & P bags on the counter. Desperately, Augie tries to hoist himself out of the hole. But Dog's all over him. Its tongue is exactly one mile long, and it's dripping with a good gallon of saliva, and its breath is even worse than Edna Mae Hamblin's when she smokes.

"Get this mutt off me!" he groans as he tries to push Dog away.

"Not until you apologize," Lydie chides.

"Apologize?" he exclaims. "For what?"

"For breaking into my house," Lydie says.

"It's not your house!" he yells at her.

"Well, it's *someone's,*" she exclaims. "Thanks to you they don't have a kitchen floor anymore." She opens a box of cereal and pours herself a handful. "You want some Cheerios?" she asks.

"I want out of this hole!" he pleads. "I want you to call your mutt off of me!"

Shrugging, she tosses the Cheerios in a bowl and puts

the bowl by the door. Evidently Dog likes Cheerios better than it likes Augie. Hearing Dog suck up the cereal is even more disgusting than smelling Dog.

He tries to unwedge himself from the hole again, but he can't make it.

"I'll help you," she says.

"Don't you bother," he tells her.

She kneels behind him and sticks her hands under his armpits. One major tug and she drags Augie out of the hole.

Once he catches his breath, he crawls around the kitchen floor, collecting all the papers that have fallen out of the suitcase, cramming them back into the suitcase. Slowly, he gets to his feet.

"I should have guessed it was you who stole my papers," Augie says.

"Talk about letdowns," she says, sighing. "All I get is Benno's report card and the pink slip Miss Merkel's sister got and traffic tickets for people I never even heard of. What do I want with their stupid secrets, Augie?"

"What did you think you'd get?"

"One of *your* secrets, Augie," she says gleefully.

"I don't have any secrets," Augie says.

"Why do you do it, Augie?"

"I'm the town snoop is all," Augie explains. "I like sticking my nose into everybody else's beeswax."

"You're lonely," she says.

"I got friends," he says.

"You feel left out of things," she says. "I know how it is. I stole the box so I'd get connected to you and it's full of stuff you stole so *you'd* feel connected."

She picks up a card and looks at it. "Not that I'd like to

be connected to the Wyatts," she says, laughing. "They got to be the dullest folks in the world, Augie."

"You give me that!" he shouts.

"You can do better," Lydie says. "Wait till the Gypsies come. You'll see. What do you want with Tommy and Debbie and Bobby and Laurel? They look like creeps to me."

"They're not creeps. They're normal!" Augie exclaims. "Don't you ever wish you were normal?"

"Me?" Lydie asks, laughing. "Normal would be a major step down for me, don't you think?"

Augie slams the suitcase shut. Stepping around the hole in the floor, he starts for the door. Before he gets there, she lurches toward him and grabs the suitcase out of his grasp. "Show me your little hand, Augie," she says.

"My hand?" he asks so softly, he can barely hear himself say it. "It's not a secret."

"You keep it hidden in the glove," she says. "If you want your suitcase back, you got to show it to me."

"You stop that, Lydie," he says. "You keep the suitcase, for all I care."

The trike lies on its side. The handlebar is twisted out of shape; the spokes are broken. The tires have been ripped to shreds.

Augie manages to get it back on its three wheels, but it's clear no one will ride this honey again. He grabs the handlebar with his good hand and starts to walk the trike back to Mrs. Lumaghi's.

"What color eyes did my grandparents have?" Augie asks.

"Who wants to know?" Uncle Emil asks.

"It's for school," Augie explains.

Honey spoons out a green pepper and puts it on Augie's plate. "Why would Miss Merkel care about something like that?" she asks.

"My science paper is genetics," Augie explains. "It's due tomorrow." As he takes a bite of the stuffed pepper, he feels the steam on his face.

"Genetics?" she asks, still smiling. "Don't you have to wait till high school for that?"

"It's no big deal. Just a map," Augie says. "It's why I have black hair, and brown eyes."

"They make everyone do a map?" she asks. "What if you're adopted?"

"But I'm not adopted," Augie reminds her. "Did you know black hair is dominant?"

Honey shakes her head. "So?"

"So probably your folks both had blond hair," Augie says. "Or you wouldn't be blond, too. Blond's recessive."

"So?"

Sometimes she just pretends she doesn't get it, Augie decides. No one's this dim!

"But black hair like mine is dominant," he continues. "So are brown eyes. I don't know about funny hands. They're probably recessive. What do you think, Honey?"

"How would I know about things like that?" she asks.

"You went to school," he says.

"They didn't have genetics back then," Honey says.

"They had photos," Augie says. "That picture was of my dad, wasn't it?"

"I don't remember any photo," she says.

"You kept it hidden in the kitchen drawer," he says. "When I found it, you took it away. Why can't I see it?"

Honey takes another forkful of stuffed pepper. But her eyes are tearing up already. She coughs. She spits a mouthful of rice and ground beef and pepper skin into her napkin. Still coughing, she runs from the room.

"You made her cry, Augie," Uncle Emil says.

"I want to see my dad, is all," Augie protests.

"Why?" Uncle Emil asks him. "Why do you have to see him?"

"It's like those stars you want to see during the daytime," Augie says. "Some things you just got to see to believe."

Chapter Twenty-Three

WHEN HE SLEEPS, he dreams. It's night. He's outside. At first he thinks he's at the top of the ridge behind his house, but he's not. It's nothing like Warsaw Junction.

He sees a campfire in the distance. Someone is playing a violin. Strange music to a plaintive tempo that Augie has never heard before. He hears the men's laughter. How can they joke when the music is so sad?

Augie steps closer to the campfire. Where are the men? Where is the music coming from?

The ground shakes. A horse whinnies. In the moonlight he sees the stallion galloping across the desert. A rider sits high in the saddle. When he tugs at the reins, the horse's forelegs rise into the air. Whinnying mightily, the horse dances on its rear legs, stopping only a few feet from the fire. As the rider dismounts, his wide-brimmed hat, secured by a string, slips down between his shoulders.

He slaps the horse's haunch hard. The horse whinnies again and disappears into the dark. The rider pushes the jet-black hair away from his eyes.

Augie sees the ring the man wears in his ear. It's gold. Even in the moonlight, he never saw anything shine so bright.

The man's eyes wander over the landscape. Augie can tell he's searching for something.

"I'm here!" Augie says.

But the man doesn't seem to hear him, either.

"I'm here!" Augie shouts. "I'm here, Dad!"

The man steps back into the shadows.

Augie starts running. But no matter how fast he runs, how loud he shouts, the man evaporates, right into thin . . .

Chapter Twenty-Four

THE NEXT morning, he sees his PC is still on. How did he manage to forget to turn his computer off the night before, he wonders. He checks the monitor screen. His genetic map is as ready as it will ever be, he figures. All he has to do is run it off on the printer.

He keys "EXIT."

"Save document? (Y/N?)"

"N." The map disappears.

As he turns the machine off, he remembers the Gypsies.

"Please," he whispers. "You've got to come for me."

Chapter Twenty-Five

WHEN AUGIE shows up on the Warnkes' doorstep, Kyle and his dad are fighting again. Augie doesn't even bother to knock. He just bides his time till Kyle comes storming out of the house.

"What's it this time?" Augie asks. "Is it still that dumb dinner you don't want to go to?"

"It's my allowance," Kyle says as he tears down the steps.

"What happened to the Beavers' dinner?" Augie asks as he catches up. "Did you get Ulee to go?"

"No, I'm going." Kyle groans.

"How come you gave in?"

"Denny's going, and so is Benno," Kyle says. "I didn't want to be the only kid who wasn't going."

"I'm not," Augie says.

"But no one's expecting you to be there," Kyle says impatiently. "It's a father-and-son thing."

As Augie follows Kyle down the steps, he notices the Warnkes' mailbox. "You ever wonder how that happened?" Augie asks, pointing to the dent in it.

Kyle shakes his head. "You're probably the only one who even noticed it."

The boys are at their usual table in the cafeteria. As Ginger walks by with her tray, it's hard to avoid the fat grin on her face.

"What's she so happy about?" Kyle asks.

"I hear one of her uncles is up for parole," Denny says.

The kids laugh.

"Maybe somebody died," Jan Prokash says.

The kids laugh even harder.

"What do you think's going on with her, Augie?" Kyle asks.

Augie shrugs.

"Come on, Augie," Denny says. "It's your turn!"

"Why don't you guys just leave her alone for once?" Augie says.

He takes the shortcut through Frick Park. If you want to see infrastructure on the skids, this is the place. The walks are rutted, and the gardens haven't been tended as far back as Augie can remember.

He hears kids cheering on the diamond. Little League practice is just breaking up. Automatically he walks faster, hoping to pass the fountain before anyone notices him.

He walks along Main Street. He sees an envelope lying in the gutter. He kicks a leaf away. Just some paper. Big deal. Who cares?

That afternoon, Mr. Krulis drops by the laundry. "You okay, Augie?" he asks.

"You know something I don't?"

"I saw the trike in the alley," Mr. Krulis says.

"Just an accident," Augie says, shrugging. "There's nothing to worry about."

Not that he thinks Mr. Krulis was worried. It's just he has to talk about something when he comes in for his laundry. "The trike's totaled," Mr. Krulis says. "You could have been hurt."

"I wasn't riding it," Augie explains.

"How did . . . ?"

"Some guys," Augie says. But he's looking at the dumb pin in Mr. Krulis's lapel. It's one of those Beaver pins. It's gold, but the beaver is red and it's got these big enamel teeth on it.

It's every bit as dumb as Kyle said.

Chapter Twenty-Six

HIS MOM is on the phone when he gets home. Augie assumes she's talking to her friend Trish because that's who she talks to mostly.

"You want to go to the Beavers' Banquet?" Honey asks, holding her hand over the receiver.

"Since when did they let Trish into the Beavers?" he asks.

"Not with Trish," Honey says. "With Mr. Krulis."

"What do you want me to tell him?" Augie asks anxiously.

"What do I know about guy stuff?" she asks, holding the phone out to him. "It's him on the phone."

Augie cautiously takes the phone from her.

Chapter Twenty-Seven

"I HEAR you're going to the Beavers' Banquet," Kyle says the day after on their way to school.

"Well, everyone else is going," Augie explains. "Besides, my mom said I had to."

Chapter Twenty-Eight

WHEN AUGIE comes into class, he notices the stack of papers on Miss Merkel's desk. It's the genetics assignments. He can see a big red B+ on the top paper, but he can't see whose paper it is.

All he knows is it's not his.

Almost as soon as he reaches his desk, the bell rings. The class rises for the Pledge of Allegiance. He places his hand over his heart like he's supposed to, but he barely mumbles the words.

He expects Miss Merkel to hand back the papers first thing. But thanks to the flu epidemic last January, the class is still two weeks behind in American history.

The first order of business that morning is the Gilded Age. Even if Augie isn't too excited about history, the Gilded Age gives him a little more time to come up with a decent excuse.

If they had a dog, Augie could say it ate the homework. But Uncle Emil has asthma, so they don't have a dog. He's got to come up with something else.

Two rows ahead, Benno Kelly is reading a comic book.

Cupper Marks is relaying a note from Bren Woody to Mina Wejchert.

Denny is making spitballs. He's a good shot, too. Trouble is, most of the kids don't even notice when Denny gets them in the back of their heads.

He could say they had to take Uncle Emil to the ER for his asthma. It could happen. They did that about a year ago, once. Miss Merkel closes the history text. She reaches for the stack of papers on the filing cabinet. As she leafs through them, she smiles.

"Did you pass everyone this time?" E. Banacek asks.

"Everyone who turned something in," she says. "You did a nice job here." She drops a blue folder on E.'s desk. "You too, Benno," she adds as she hands him his paper.

Augie sees the C+ on Benno's paper. He sees the frown on Benno's face, too. Apparently, Miss Merkel thinks more of a C+ than Benno does.

"Not bad."

"Good job."

"Nice job."

"Good."

"Okay."

Miss Merkel pauses at Lydie's desk. "What happened?" she asks.

"Oh, I got busy," Lydie says cheerfully. "Personal stuff. You know how it is."

"You should have asked for an extension," Miss Merkel tells her.

"To tell you the truth," Lydie continues, "genetics just isn't my thing. Is that going to be a problem, Miss Merkel?"

"Only if you're planning on seventh grade next

September," Miss Merkel says, walking toward the back of the class.

Augie can see the kids turning, raising their eyebrows significantly. Some of them are giggling. Not Augie. He knows something is up. It's too much of a coincidence, him and Lydie screwing up on the same assignment.

Miss Merkel starts down the last aisle.

"Very nice."

"Good."

As she steps closer, he decides on the asthma. But he won't say it's Uncle Emil's. He'll say it's because he has asthma. He'll ask for the extension, too.

"Excellent, Augie," Miss Merkel says.

As she lays the blue folder on his desk, he notices the big red A+.

"Very original," Mrs. Merkel tells him. "Did your PC break down?"

He folds back the cover. It's her handwriting. Same as her note that he found in the laundry. What the heck is Lydie Rose up to now? he wonders. Even for her, this is weird.

"Augie?" Miss Merkel asks. "Would you like to read it to the class?"

The chairs scrape against the linoleum as the kids turn to look.

"Stand up, Augie," Miss Merkel says, "so everyone can hear you better."

Augie gets to his feet. He's got to read this like it's not the first time he ever saw these words. He turns over the cover. Right away, an alarm goes off in his head.

"'Mutant Pioneers,'" he reads, but mostly it's a mumble.

"Did you say what I think you said?" Denny asks.

"The title is 'Mutant Pioneers,'" Miss Merkel says. "Better speak up, Augie."

"That's a weird title," Cupper Marks says.

"It's an excellent title," Lydie says. "That's what kind of title it is."

"Please, Lydie."

"But what's it supposed to mean?" Denny asks.

"If you'd shut up for a second, you might find out!" Lydie shouts. "Doesn't anyone around here want to learn something?"

"At least I turned in my assignment, Lydie," Cupper shouts back.

"Girls!"

"Yes, Miss Merkel."

"Yes, Miss Merkel."

"Augie, please."

"'When you see someone on the street with their elbow growing out of the wrong place . . . ,'" he reads out loud.

(He reads it again to himself. An elbow growing out of the wrong place? What is *that* supposed to mean?)

"Please, Augie," Miss Merkel says. "Go on."

His hand is shaking so hard, he can barely read the handwriting, big though it is. He feels the blood pounding in his neck.

"Augie?"

He looks around at the kids. Ginger, Benno, Kyle, Denny—all of them—are shaking their heads. Bren Goody and Cupper Marks are raising their eyebrows like they're listening to some crazy person.

"Well, I'm not an expert on term papers," Lydie

Rose says, "but if that's not a great opening, I don't know what is!"

Augie's legs are so wobbly now, he can barely stand up. "I can't," he says. "I can't."

As soon as the bell rings, he runs down the hall, still clutching the term paper. As soon as he reaches the faculty lounge, he's going to destroy it. The room is empty. He's relieved. When he hears the door behind him squeak open, he turns.

"Get out of here," he tells her.

"A-plus!" Lydie Rose exclaims. "Some thanks I get."

"Why me, Lydie Rose?" he asks. "Why can't you pick on someone else?"

"Those other kids?" she laughs scornfully. "Most of them don't have one single thing that makes them stand out."

"They're not mutants," he says. "That's what you mean."

"Why, Augie!" she exclaims. "That's it exactly!" Suddenly she grabs for the hand with the glove.

He pulls his hand away. "I'm going to the Beavers' Banquet," he tells her.

"What's that supposed to mean?" she asks.

"From now on, you're the only mutant around here," he says. "That's what it means."

Chapter Twenty-Nine

HONEY OFFERS to drive him downtown, but he walks instead. What's he want a mom for the night of the Beavers' Father-Son Banquet, anyway? It's almost evening, but the sun's just setting, and it's still warm out.

As Augie walks along Hannah Avenue, he sees old Mrs. Sykes rocking on her porch and the Gertz twins next door playing tag in their driveway. Someone's running their lawn mower. First time this spring. Must be Mr. Loucks. He's famous in the neighborhood for mowing his lawn at night.

He turns right on Main Street. The stores are all closed now. He passes Mrs. Lumaghi's. The lights are off and the door's locked. But he can see the glow coming from the back. It's her TV. She's still at it. He wonders what she watches when the daytime talk shows are over.

Mozart Hall is at the end of the block. Everyone's there, just like he expected, hanging around out front on the sidewalk. Benno, Marty, Brad, Kiefer, even Blue.

The kids are all wearing their regular school clothes. Augie slips off the blazer that Honey made him wear and slings it over his shoulder. If there were time, he'd run home and change his flannel pants for some jeans.

Not all the kids are with their dads, either. Benno Kelly is with his stepdad, and Neal Socci is standing next to his grandfather. Neal Gordon is there with his older brother.

(Okay, so no one else is here with their mom's boyfriend, but Augie doesn't care. Besides, you never know. Next year Honey and Mr. Krulis could be more than friends.)

No one flashed the light. No bell went off. But everyone's starting up the steps now. Augie scans the crowd again. Kyle and his dad are on the other side of the steps. Augie pushes his way through the crowd toward them.

"You seen Mr. Krulis?" he asks Kyle's father.

"Not yet," Mr. Warnke says. "Probably had to stay late at the store."

Augie nods, even though he just passed Krulis-Hallmark and it was all closed up. As the men and the boys walk into the building, Augie steps aside to let them pass.

He looks down Main Street. The sidewalks are empty. He checks his watch. It's only a few minutes after seven.

Sitting down on the cement steps outside the hall, he watches the men and boys disappear into the building. The clock in the steeple of the Methodist Church at the end of the street begins to chime.

One, two, three.

Too impatient to count anymore, Augie looks at his watch again. Mr. Krulis is hardly late yet, but Augie can't help it. He's nervous.

Augie hears a door slam behind him.

"Hey, Augie."

As he turns, he sees Kyle stepping toward him.

"Yeah?"

"My dad says you should sit with us," Kyle tells him.

"I'm sitting with Mr. Krulis."

"You're sitting outside alone."

"So he's a little late," Augie says, shrugging.

"Well, just in case you change your mind."

Augie notices a car down the block, parked in front of the Methodist Church. It's a Volvo. A yellow, late-model Volvo. The parking lights are on, too.

Quickly, Augie gets to his feet. What's Mr. Krulis waiting in his car for? he wonders.

He runs down the block, past the shoe repair, and the movie theater where there aren't any movies, past the pharmacy. The car is on the other side of the street. Without looking right or left, he runs across the street.

"Mr. Krulis!" he shouts.

But the car is empty. He pulls the handle. The door is locked. Something is wrong. You don't lock up your car and leave the parking lights on.

"Mr. Krulis?" he calls out. "Where are you, Mr. Krulis?"

Next to the church is the graveyard. A tall, wrought-iron fence runs around it. Sticking his head between two of the posts, Augie peers inside. It's like a little park, with trees, and grass, and a white gravel path running through it.

Plus graves, all lined up in neat rows. There're bouquets of flowers, mostly daffodils, on some of the graves. Sometimes the flowers are plastic. Hesitantly, Augie pushes the gate open just wide enough for him to step inside.

It's not spooky. Just quiet. Except for the breeze rustling through the trees, the place is absolutely still. Every time Augie takes a step, the gravel crunches. Except for some birds, it's the only noise there.

He can't have gone more than twenty or thirty feet before he sees the man sitting on a cement bench. Even if his head is buried in his hands, Augie knows it's got to be him. "Mr. Krulis?" Augie whispers.

The man raises his head slowly. "Oh, it's you, Augie," he says.

"I saw your car," Augie says.

"Yeah?"

"I was looking for you," Augie says.

"Is something wrong?" Mr. Krulis asks.

"It's the Beavers' Banquet," Augie explains. "We've got to hurry, Mr. Krulis, or we'll be late for the Father-Son Banquet."

Mr. Krulis points to a marble slab in the grass. "Look, Augie. That's him."

"Who, Mr. Krulis?"

But Mr. Krulis doesn't say anything. He just keeping pointing. So Augie looks, even though he doesn't want to. What else can he do?

James Krulis
1985–2000

"That's my little boy," Mr. Krulis says, his voice cracking.

Next to it is another marble slab. For Beverly Krulis. 1962–2000. Mr. Krulis's wife, he figures.

"I'm sorry," Augie murmurs.

"For what?" Mr. Krulis asks. "What do you have to be sorry for?"

"I'm sorry they died," Augie says.

"Me too," Mr. Krulis says sadly. "Me too."

"You want me to wait outside?"

"Wait?"

"Till you want to go to the Beavers' Banquet," Augie says.

"Oh, I don't know about that," Mr. Krulis says.

"But you asked me," Augie protests.

"It's Jimmy I should be taking with me," Mr. Krulis says. "Not you, Augie."

Augie sees the tears streaming down Mr. Krulis's face. He knows he's supposed to feel sorry for him, but he doesn't. "I told all the kids I was going with you," he tells Mr. Krulis. "They saw me out there, waiting for you."

"You want me to say I'm sorry?" Mr. Krulis asks. "Is that what you want me to say, Augie?"

As Augie steps back, the gravel crunches under his feet. "It's not like you're my father," he says angrily. "You don't have to say a thing."

As Mr. Krulis gets to his feet, Augie breaks into a run. "Hey, wait, Augie," Mr. Krulis pleads. "You got to understand."

Augie tears down the path toward the street. He pushes the gate open. The jacket catches on one of the iron points. Augie gives the jacket a tug. The fabric rips. Letting go of the coat, he slams the gate shut. What's he need a blazer for anyway?

Chapter Thirty

THE STREET'S deserted. All he hears are his own footsteps as he runs down the center of Main Street. When he glances over his shoulder, he sees the car, one headlight on, moving slowly along the street behind him.

It's her jalopy. Even in the twilight, he recognizes her behind the wheel. Dog sits up straight next to her in the passenger seat. Radar, he wonders. Is *that* how she does it? Did she implant computer chips in his skull that send out signals at exactly those times he can least stand to see her? He turns at the corner at Hannah. He doesn't look back again, but he can feel her coming alongside.

"So how was the Beavers' Banquet?"

"It was fabulous," he snorts. "Soup-to-nuts fabulous."

"Over a little early, isn't it?"

"Depends on how you look at it," he says, still running.

"You want to get in?" she asks, bringing the jalopy to a clattering halt.

"Thanks but no thanks," he says, pausing to catch his breath.

"I got something to cheer you up," she says brightly.

"Don't need cheering up," he insists.

"Sure you do," she says.

"Don't!" he snaps.

He starts walking along the street.

"It's your dumb suitcase," she sings out. "You can have it back."

As he turns, he sees her hoisting it over the door.

"You probably stole half the things in it," he groans.

"Just the Wyatts' Christmas card," Lydie says. "I just couldn't bear to part with Clem."

As he reaches out for the suitcase, she drops it on the pavement, grabbing for his gloved hand.

"Don't!" Augie shouts, pulling his hand away.

"Aw, come on, Augie," Lydie pleads. "I just want to hold it."

"You're disgusting!"

"The Gypsies are going to love your little hand," Lydie says. "They'll show you how special you are, Augie. It's something to celebrate."

He holds his hand up to her face. "Celebrate this? I hate this. I hate this every day."

"You don't mean that," Lydie protests. "When the Gypsies come, you'll understand."

"Don't you get it, Lydie? They never come for gimps like me."

He picks up the suitcase and he starts running. As he turns the last corner, he sees the porch light is on.

"Hey, Augie, don't give up on the Gypsies," Lydie shouts.

But he's not listening to her anymore. The pain in him is too loud. It's ripping him up inside.

Clutching the suitcase to his chest, he runs across the backyard, runs past Uncle Emil's ditch. He swings the barn door open and runs inside. He skirts the beams and shingles that have collected since the roof caved in and he races toward the stalls.

He doesn't stop till he comes to the last one. His fury still building, he raises his gloved hand. With all his might he slams his mutated hand against the rough timber, over and over, till splinters tear through the glove.

"I hate you!" he cries. "I hate you!"

He feels the splintered wood tearing at his flesh, but still he keeps pounding the wall, harder and harder. The blood from the injured hand seeps through the fabric, but Augie doesn't stop hitting the timber until the glove is covered with his blood.

He collapses to the ground. He feels the barn enveloping him with its soft, sweet smell of hay and timber.

"I hate you, Lydie Rose Meisenheimer!" he whispers. "I hate you and your Gypsies!"

He'd shout it, but he's too tired. Still sobbing, he lets the exhaustion take him.

Chapter Thirty-One

IT'S NIGHT.

He's heard something, but he doesn't know what. Music, maybe. Maybe not. With his good hand, he brushes the straw from his hair. Quickly he gets to his feet. He doesn't hear it now, but someone's there. He knows it.

He's got to get out of here, and he's got to take the suitcase with him. He knows it's not safe here. He clasps the handle and tries to pick it up. When did it get to be so heavy? He drags it past the stalls. Lugs it over the debris and out of the barn.

The sky is all stars tonight. As he looks up, he sees them twinkling through the branches of the locust trees.

"Augie!"

Augie whirls around on his heels. "Mom?" he calls out.

But the backyard is still. All he hears is the breeze rustling through the trees.

"I know it's you, Kyle," he announces, "so don't think you're scaring me any!"

"Over here!"

It could be coming from the ditch. Augie steps toward the edge of it. "Uncle Emil?" he whispers.

His shoe hits a rock. How could he have even noticed it in the moonlight? He stumbles. He tries to recover his balance, but too late. As he goes sprawling, the suitcase flies out of his grasp.

He watches it soar into the air. As it crashes into the dirt, the lock breaks. The suitcase springs open, disgorging its contents all along the periphery of Uncle Emil's ditch.

He kneels in the dirt, desperately trying to retrieve it all. But everything's all torn now, covered with dirt. It's taken him forever to collect it all . . . and now it's just junk.

He's mad now. What was the point of collecting it, he wonders. He sees the essay Lydie Rose handed in for him. It's smeared with dirt. He'd like nothing more than to tear it into a million pieces, but how can he do that with just one hand?

He spots the matches Mr. Fountain left in the faculty lounge john. On the inside front cover are two handwritten telephone numbers. Augie's been meaning to call them someday, but he doesn't care about that now. If he rests the gloved hand over one end of the matchbook, he can try to light the matches with his good hand.

The first two matches are duds. Too damp. The third struggles to life. Before it goes out, Augie sticks the edge of Lydie Rose's note into the flame. It catches! In only a few seconds the fire swarms over the paper, charring the edges, sending little sparks flying into the air.

It's too hot for Augie to hold. The paper floats down into the hole. The flames ebb. If he doesn't feed the fire right away, it's going to die!

Grabbing more papers, he hurls them into the hole. So

what if he meant to keep them forever? All that matters now is keeping that fire going! Mrs. Merkel's sister's pink slip from the telephone company and Benno Kelly's report card ignite almost as soon as they land. Augie grabs Gray Dmytryck's letter and tosses it into the fire, too. Ticket stubs, postcards from Florida, shopping lists—they're all burning now.

Only the suitcase is left. Augie hurls it into the pit. The flame catches the old leather immediately, engulfing the ditch with fire, filling the air with strange music. The fire crackles rhythmically. It sounds almost like horse's hoofs galloping across the desert.

"Augie."

Slowly, Augie looks over his shoulder. A man stands behind him. His face is illuminated by the flames. The square chin, the dark eyes, the black hair that falls across his forehead. Augie remembers the man. He's seen him once before.

"Go away!" Augie says, turning back to the fire.

The man sits down next to him at the edge of the hole. "What are you burning?" he asks.

Augie shrugs. "Just stuff," he murmurs.

"What type stuff?"

"None of your business type stuff," Augie says.

The man smiles. "Oh, that kind of stuff."

When he rests a hand on Augie's shoulder, Augie pulls away. The man doesn't seem to notice.

Augie watches as the man's eyes fall on the glove. Augie's hand spasms. Instinctively Augie hides his hand under his butt.

"Let me see it, Augie," he says.

Reluctantly, Augie holds up his hand.

"Without the glove."

Augie shakes his head. "No." He sighs.

The man takes Augie's wrist in one hand. With the other, he tugs gently at the cotton-filled fingers, one by one. The little lump of flesh is covered with dried blood. "Why, Augie?" he asks. "How did you hurt your little hand?"

"That's none of your business, too," Augie declares.

The man reaches for the canteen hanging from his belt. He unscrews the cap. Tenderly, he washes the blood and grime from the little lump of flesh. He removes the red kerchief from his neck and dries the little hand with it.

The shredded glove lies in the earth, caked with dirt and blood. Augie reaches for it with his good hand.

"What do you want with that?" the man asks.

"I need it," Augie explains.

The man shakes his head. He draws Augie's little hand to his face. Augie can feel the coarseness of the man's beard on the back of his little hand.

"No!" Augie protests.

He feels the man kissing the little stumps of flesh, one by one. But he doesn't protest anymore. He doesn't pull away.

"The glove, Augie," the man says to him.

"I'm scared!"

"Now. Before the flame dies."

The fire is devouring the suitcase now. Quickly, Augie hurls the glove into the flames. The fire crackles. The embers glow. In only a few seconds, the glove is ashes.

Chapter Thirty-Two

IT'S SATURDAY, but the alarm goes off, anyway. If he's late one more time for Mrs. Lumaghi, she's going to let him have it.

His jeans are lying on the floor by the dresser; his T-shirt is hanging over the back of the chair. One sneaker is on the floor of the closet. The other is on top of his PC.

His watch is on the bed table. It's the only thing that's where it's supposed to be. As he straps it on, he looks for his glove. He checks behind the lamp, then under the bed. He checks the pockets of his jeans, but all he finds is a red kerchief.

As soon as he's dressed, he races down the stairs.

His mom's got the phone cradled between her neck and her shoulder so she can talk and rinse the dishes at the same time. "It's Harv," she says, holding the phone up. "He wants to make it up to you."

"Anything but the Beavers."

"How about a Pirates game in Pittsburgh?" Honey asks.

"How about Six Flags?"

While his mom talks to Harv, Augie chugs the orange

juice. As he bites into a doughnut, he notices his hand. He remembers last night—that part of it, anyway. He doesn't remember after, though.

"What happened to your glove?" Honey asks, still on the phone. "You lose the one I made you last week?"

"I guess I lost it," he says, shrugging. "I can't remember."

"I'll fix you a new one."

"No big deal," Augie says, already out the door.

The day's turning into a scorcher, but Uncle Emil is already digging away in his pit.

"You see any stars yet this morning?" Augie asks.

"Just this mess," Uncle Emil says, pointing to a heap of ashes at the very bottom of the hole.

Augie peers into the pit. He can hardly believe the pile of ashes he sees. "Someone having a barbecue?" he asks as he scratches his head.

"Probably those kids up the hill," Emil says. "Who knows what they were up to this time!"

Inside the barn is the new trike. Mrs. Lumaghi's son has rigged up the cage for the laundry so it looks just as tacky as the old one.

Rudy made the sign, too.

Lumaghi Cleaners
Free Delivery
555-3291

The letters are still red and green on a white background, same colors as the Italian flag.

As Augie pedals the trike downtown, he sees old Mr. Loucks, waiting at the corner for the light to change. "Hey, Augie, you know if I can get me some extra cheese on my dry cleaning?" he asks.

"Yeah, but it's a nickel," he says cheerfully.

As Mr. Loucks slaps his knee, some pink paper slips out of his back pocket. Pink's promising. Could be a summons or something, Augie knows.

Augie gets off the trike and picks the paper up from the curb. "Hey, Mr. Loucks," he says. "You dropped something."

"Oh, thanks, Augie," Mr. Loucks says. "How about anchovies, Augie? How much extra's that?"

"For anchovies, you'd better try Minnie's Martinizing," Augie says.

Lydie Rose's so-called convertible is parked down the block. Something's up. He knows that right away. The seats are piled high with junk: cardboard boxes overflowing with old clothes, a TV set with a busted screen, an old rocking chair, even a rusted water heater.

As Augie brings the trike to a stop, he sees her coming out of Mrs. Lumaghi's. As usual, the black straw hat covers most of her face. This morning, her dress is a jungle print, complete with lions and tigers and an elephant. Even Mrs. Lumaghi's old lady friends wouldn't wear anything *that* ugly.

Her arms are piled so high with plastic bags that she can't even see him standing a few feet away from her. He waits till she dumps the laundry on top of the rest of her junk.

"Come to say good-bye?" he asks.

At the sound of his voice, she jumps. "I never was much for the good-bye part."

"Why?" he asks. "*Why* are you going, Lydie?"

"It's what I do, I guess."

It takes some maneuvering but Lydie finally clears away enough junk so she can sit in the driver's seat. Her eyes linger a moment on his little hand. For once, though, she doesn't speak.

"It's okay if you want to look at it," he tells her.

As he holds his arm out to her, she examines the little pink hand.

"It's really so cool," she says admiringly.

"I guess it is, sort of," he admits.

"You'd better take good care of it, Augie."

"Like it was one of the family," Augie says.

Laughing, she turns the key in the ignition. The car backfires twice. "Hey, Augie, you wouldn't have the time, would you?" Lydie asks.

Augie checks his wrist. It's gone! When he looks up, he sees her dangling the watch in the air. She's grinning, too.

"Hey! You give me my watch back!" he shouts.

"No way!" she laughs as the car lurches down Main Street.

Augie runs after her. "You come back with my watch!" he shouts. "You come back, you Gypsy!"

The car picks up speed. So does Augie. For a whole block he runs after her. But it's no use. No matter how fast he runs, he's no match for Lydie Rose's so-called car.

Still gasping for air, he staggers to a stop and wipes the sweat from his face. Lydie's car disappears around the corner. He sticks his new red kerchief back into his pocket and walks back toward the store.

He sees Mrs. Lumaghi out on the sidewalk, hanging dry cleaning in the back of Augie's trike. "Looks like you got yourself a new friend," she says.

Somehow Dog's crawled into the cage. It's lying on its side, snoring away. Augie watches its mangy old stomach heave up and down.

"I guess the Gypsies didn't come for it, either," Augie says.

"What Gypsies?" Mrs. Lumaghi asks. "We ain't got no Gypsies around here."

But Augie's checking the addresses on the cleaning, figuring out his route. First stop will be Miss Meyer, over on Mission Lane. Then the Novaks, on Fourth Street. Then Mr. Bourne.

"If you want to get rid of that smelly old fleabag, you'd better wake it up first," Mrs. Lumaghi says.

"Let it sleep," Augie says, getting on the trike.

With Dog snoring away back in the cage, Augie starts pedaling the trike down Main Street.

Appendix

Mutant Pioneers

BY *Augie Knapp*

When you see someone on the street with their elbow growing out of the wrong place, or maybe they were born missing something, you're just glad it didn't happen to you. Some people call them freaks, but I say they are unsung heroes!

If some fish didn't have a mutation that let it breathe out of water and some other fish didn't have a foot growing out of one of its fins, we'd still be living in the sea. Personally, I can think of several things we'd be better off without. And maybe your elbow *should* be someplace else.

Who knows what human beings will look like in a million years? But if we ever breathe on Mars, if everyone starts getting along with everyone else, we'll probably have some mutant to thank for it.

Plenty of scientists didn't find the Salk vaccine, but they are still counted as medical pioneers. Christopher Columbus never did get to India, you know, and every year he gets a parade.